Wives Who Love Women

Wives Who Love Women

By JANE SCOTT

WALKER AND COMPANY
New York

First published in the United States of America in 1978 by the Walker Publishing Company, Inc.

Published simultaneously in Canada by Beaverbooks, Limited, Pickering, Ontario.

ISBN: 0-8027-0597-9

Library of Congress Catalog Card Number: 77-91905

Printed in the United States of America

10 9 8 7 6 5 4 3 2 1

TO AMY

Introduction

Kicking off my bedroom slippers, I step up on my bed to draw the drapes closed, noticing as I do so that the young people next door — and there seem to be so many of them living there, eight or ten at least — are out in their backyard again, as they so often are, talking, laughing, rough-housing, listening to stereo rock music blasting out. It is early afternoon and I wonder whether those youngsters, if they should happen to glance over this way, would be able to tell what I'm doing.

Once the drapes are closed, I haul up a heavy gray blanket, pin it over the drapes, then finish off with a light orange spread, bunching it in above the rod to shut out the last faint glimmers of exterior light. If those playful youngsters next door do notice the way I frequently black out my room this way, what in the world do they make of it?

Surely — a generation older than they — I appear to them as just another respectable, middle-aged wife and mother, so I doubt it would even cross their minds that I do this in order to enjoy a lesbian love affair.

I darken the room because Amy, my adored, adorable

Amy, self-conscious about stretch marks and an abdominal scar, likes to make love only in a very dark room, and whatever Amy wants is fine with me.

Whenever she is due over—we time it for early afternoon, after the start of fifth-period class at the local high school—I shower, pin up the blanket, carefully lock three of the four doors into the house, then meet Amy at the front door, wearing only my shorty robe. After a quick warm kiss, we lock the front door and hurry down the hall to my bedroom, where Amy quickly undresses—and what a thrill this gives me, that my love is so eager and well trained! I toss off my robe, and within sixty seconds of her arrival we are climbing nude into bed, two fifty-year-old, married grandmothers bursting with joy because we have found and are daring to love each other.

This is how it happened.

One

The room was small, only about twelve by twenty feet, overcrowded with frayed, dumpy, overstuffed furniture. As I entered I noticed an empty stool in the far corner and headed straight for it. It wasn't until I had claimed my spot on the stool that I dared look around.

There were five other women present, settled on the various tattered, innard-bleeding sofas and chairs, and as I glanced around my heart plunged: they were all so young! Over the phone this afternoon, when I'd talked to a woman about possibly attending this rap tonight, I'd asked her pointedly if all the women were young, and she'd assured me, "Oh, no, they aren't, certainly not. A lot of the women are thirty or more." She'd added rather breathlessly, "Some are even in their forties." How about fifty? I had wanted to counter, but the way she'd made forty sound ancient and toothless disheartened me too thoroughly to question her further.

Hanging up, I'd felt unsure as to whether I really wanted to go. At the Gay Community Services Center in Los Angeles, which I'd doggedly attended week after week the year before, three-quarters of those in attendance had been well under thirty. For the most part the rap sessions had bored me silly, and not once had I met a single woman of any age toward whom I'd felt anything more than the mildest interest. I don't know what prompted me to seek out another group, yet I knew that I would go, at least once; and deep inside something cried out excitedly, Surely this time, this time . . .

I was happily married, settled, a homebody at heart, and I didn't really enjoy going out at night, besides which there was always some slight guilt whenever I went chasing off by myself to mingle with lesbians, among whom I had no very compelling reason to believe I belonged. When heading toward a rap session, I customarily slipped off my wedding ring and hid it in my purse, not wanting it to be generally known that I had a live, warm, loving husband with whom I lived in affectionate harmony. "And what if you do find some woman," my friend Pat kept throwing at me, trying to make me come to my senses, "then what?"

I didn't know the answer; I knew only that there was a hunger in me that ached to be fed. A lifetime before, during my teen-age years, I'd sought out the homosexual world, had felt that, as fond as I was of women and as little as I felt attracted to men, I must surely be a lesbian. By the age of twenty, however, I had backed out of that world, unable to adjust to it, unable to shed my inhibitions sufficiently to become sexually involved. I had felt no conscious sexual desire for women.

By my mid-twenties I had decided that, just as many people seem to be repressed homosexuals, I was a repressed heterosexual. Whenever I'd have a few drinks—this was back in my salad days, before I became the teetotaler I've been for the past twenty years—I'd invariably head toward the nearest male to flirt; the few sexual dreams I had were exclusively heterosexual; I'd felt happy and secure those few times I had allowed myself the luxury of being physically, though not yet sexually, close to a male. In fact, the push toward heterosexuality seemed so strong, and I so unequivocally wanted to have a child, that in time I plunged headlong into marriage with much the same determination that someone panicked by water might force himself to jump into a pool.

Jump, dammit, jump! I ordered myself. And, plunging in, I figured in short order I'd either sink or learn to swim.

Fortunately, despite some acute sexual problems at the very beginning, I learned to swim. I married a newly divorced man, Russell Scott, who was ten years older than I and had three young sons, and, as the fairy tales have it, we lived happily ever after.

That is to say, we had frequent, furious fights, often wishing to hell we'd never met much less married each other, on occasion bitterly regretting that we couldn't afford a divorce. But, trapped by our abiding love for the children, by numerous bills, by our freely given vows to put up with each other until death intervened, we stayed together, slugging and sweating it out, and slowly over the years grew into greater understanding, acceptance, and trust. By the time we'd been married fifteen years, the angry upheavals were few and far between and the yoke of marital unity was comfortable and light; we jogged along happily together year after year, each day more certain that this would continue until one of us died.

After twenty-three years of marriage I can still glance around at Russ and feel freshly surprised at how attractive he is. At sixty, he is still very slender and erect, quick-moving, his full head of fine dark hair only lightly streaked with gray—while at fifty I am almost completely gray—and he still has the same clear skin, the same finely cut features, the same appealing, slightly shy smile.

Of course, I can also look at him and think for the ten-thousandth time what an outrageous idiot he is, a man who, slipping into old age, has still not brought his quick, explosive temper adequately under control, who still hasn't learned to relax or to compromise, a man seemingly sustained by perpetual inner fury, who continually wastes enormous amounts of energy cursing at the world, at the morning headlines, at the people he works for and with, at the ads on the TV programs he watches in the evening, even at the programs themselves. I keep hoping that someday he'll hit the bottom of his anger and no more will boil up, but so far this hasn't happened and possibly never will. By now I'm so used to his rage I might even miss it if it ended.

Underneath all this fury, protected by all this fury, lives another Russ, a man of extreme vulnerability, of great sensitivity and sentiment, a man whose sympathies are easily touched, whose eyes frequently—far more frequently than mine—fill with tears, a man who loves me and whom I love.

Eleven months after Russ and I got married, I gave birth to our first son. From that moment on—for me, the ultimate in excitement and fulfillment—there was no way I could ever regret my decision to marry. I found motherhood the most delightful and satisfying of roles. When Jason was two, I was ready and eager to plunge into another pregnancy, hoping to have a girl this time. But at that point, already supporting four sons, beset by financial problems, Russ balked. It wasn't until Jason was five that he relented and I got pregnant again. In due time our younger son, Tommy, completed our family.

Over the years, as we'd adjusted to each other, Russ had become a better and better husband, more reasonable, somewhat less explosive, slowly growing more open and trusting. He was a loyal, loving father, always generous with money, a hard worker determined to carve out a financially secure future for us. I'd grown to have a deep, underlying respect for him; I enjoyed his company, our sex life was fine, and we lived together with ever-increasing friendliness, harmony, and good will.

"So what the hell makes you so set on messing up your

life?" my friend Pat kept snapping at me. "If you ever did find a woman lover, how could you possibly manage it?"

"Don't worry," I would snap back, with true Taurean stubbornness, "somehow I'll cope!" But would I really be able to? What *did* I think I was doing?

After my reasonably enjoyable but uneventful trips down to the L.A. Gay Community Services Center, I met a married woman, Vera, about my age, in an adult education class. We immediately embarked upon a warm and exciting friendship. When I got up my nerve one day and told her I was physically attracted to her, she withdrew, in a state of shock, dropped out of class, and publicly cut me dead the few times thereafter that I happened to run into her.

"Well, what the hell did you expect?" my friend Pat said when I told her about it. "A respectable, uptight, married woman like Vera—my God, Jane, when are you going to start showing some sense?"

Winter came and I went into hibernation, staying home with my husband and younger son, properly minding my busy, happy, respectable life, doing nothing further to throw it out of tilt. But then, all too soon, spring followed, our fruit trees began sprouting little buds up and down their skinny thrust-up branches, day after day the sky was a bright sparkling blue, and deep inside I felt that aching hunger again. In April I would be fifty, half a century old —

> Never fear, Age will catch you,
> Slow you down, ere it dispatch you
> To your long and solemn quiet . . .
> What will matter then the riot
> Of the lilacs in the wind?

On impulse one spring afternoon — a few weeks before my fiftieth birthday, haunted by the faraway sound of those wind-whipped lilacs — I phoned the Los Angeles Gay Community Services Center to ask if there was anything doing out nearer to where I lived, and was given the address and telephone number of the Orange County Gay Community Services Center. Now all I had to decide was whether or not to give it a try.

"Some are even in their forties," the young woman, Debbie, had assured me over the phone, and that's really all it took. Excitement rooted and I had to go. Somewhere in this world there just had to be a woman for me, one I could be close to, who would soothe this inner ache.

Will I meet her here, tonight? I wondered.

Once I had hurriedly crossed the small, crowded room and secured my place on the stool, I dared look around — at all the young, bland faces attached to long, young bodies. Two overstuffed sofas faced each other; on each one a young woman lounged, each wearing tight, faded blue jeans and loose T-shirt. A shorter sofa stretched out from the stool upon which I perched, and another woman, not quite as young, thirty maybe, sat there tensely. Across from us, near the door, were two chairs on either side of an end table. In one of those chairs a plump woman of about forty was stationed; in the other, a very large young woman in a green pants suit who sat staring down at the floor.

As unobtrusively as possible, I glanced around from face to face, figure to figure, as I wondered what in the world I was doing here. My friend Pat had accompanied me twice during my period of pilgrimage to the L.A. Gay Center before she'd quit in disgust, asking me how I could possibly imagine I'd meet any woman I'd care for in a place like that.

"Unless you're planning to chase after some young girl," Pat had flared angrily. "Face it, Jane. Any intelligent, stable woman our age has already settled down, carved out a life for herself, made all the friends she wants or needs. She doesn't have to hang around a place like the center, which is for kids and misfits and women in crisis, not the kind of woman you're looking for."

"How do you know what kind of woman I'm looking for?" How could Pat know, when I didn't know myself? "Who says it has to be anyone either stable or intelligent? As long as she's female —" I quipped, only half kidding.

These five women here tonight all looked to be female, but three of them were far too young, still in their early twenties, and the other two— Well, hell, what was I doing here anyway?

I realized I'd forgotten to take off my wedding ring. I caught myself nervously twisting it, thought about taking it off, then in a burst of defiance decided to leave it on. Why not?

"In the first place, if you do find some woman," Pat had warned me, "and you really dig each other, then what? You think she's going to be happy seeing you only the one night a week you can sneak out from home? Are you going to level with her and tell her you're married, or lie and sneak? Either way, you're bound to lose her. And what if Russ finds out you're fooling around like that?"

As a young woman Pat had lived as a lesbian, then at age forty had given up the gay life to marry. She had no children, didn't get along well with her husband, led what seemed to me an empty, unsatisfactory life, yet at the same time seemed rigidly stuck now in the heterosexual mold and apparently felt deeply threatened by my ill-defined reaching out. At one point, hungry for something I didn't have and feeling mildly attracted to her, I had suggested that she and I might give it a try together, but she'd recoiled instantly. "Oh, Jesus, I couldn't cope with that!" she had squealed. "No way, no way!" So we'd continued on as friends, with no apparent weakening of our lukewarm mutual affection, and I stubbornly went on with my search while she gloomily forecast doom.

As I finished my surreptitious survey of those in the room, I thought of Leslie, a young redhead whom I'd met in the class in which I'd met Vera. After Vera's abrupt withdrawal from class, Leslie had remarked to me one day, rather wistfully, that she couldn't understand it, because Vera had seemed very interested in the class and so very very fond of me. Why did I suppose she'd dropped out like that?

On impulse, I had told her the why.

"I felt physically attracted to her, which sent her into a state of shock," I supplied, already regretting, as I glanced into Leslie's suddenly excited eyes, that I had opened up to her.

"My goodness," Leslie said, then erupted into an excited little giggle. "At her age you wouldn't think she'd be so naive. After all, if she didn't feel the same, if she didn't reciprocate the feeling, all she had to do was say thank you but no thanks. It's nothing to get all upset about."

"Well, thanks for your vote of confidence, but let's not discuss it any further, all right?" I knew I had stupidly slid out onto very thin ice, but surely I could scramble back. Couldn't I?

Leslie, twenty-three years old, married, a full-time college student, began eyeing me with long, hungry stares. When I left class she'd fall into step beside me, her arm brushing mine. As we walked she'd half fall against me. She asked me please, please, please! to come to her house for lunch. After we'd eaten—two hours after—when I said I just had to leave, she pleaded with me not to. When I offered my hand and said good-bye, she bit her lip, shook her head, and refused to offer her hand in return.

"No, I don't want to shake hands, I want to hug you."

When I stepped forward to put my arms around her, she hugged me so hard I thought she might crush a rib. "Oh, I've wanted to do that for so long!" she cried. "How could Vera possibly have minded what you told her?"

Oh, God, I thought.

"You only felt that way toward Vera because you knew she'd say no!" Leslie threw at me at a subsequent encounter. "You think you want to find some woman, but what you really want is to stay safe, not get involved. I understand you, Jane — oh, do I understand you! You don't really want a flesh-and-blood lover, you just want to kick the idea around — and around and around. It makes you see yourself as young and modern and oh so liberated, but inside you're as hung up, as uptight, as narrow and rigid as Vera ever thought of being. Sure, you think you want to find a woman, but the moment you do find one, one who says yes, you'll run like hell the other way — just see if you don't. Want to bet?"

Those words of Leslie's rang in my head as I stared down at the frayed, pale blue carpeting in the Gay Center's rap room. Was she right? That had certainly been the story of my youth, when, offered love, I had repeatedly run away. Would I again? Was I only fooling myself, taking up space, wasting time, when I came to these sessions?

As I heard the footsteps of someone entering the room I glanced up at once, hopeful, but it was another very young woman, tall and broad, sloppily dressed in faded blue coveralls. Flashing out a nervous grin, she flopped down at the end of a sofa. Another woman entered, then another, another, another. At eight o'clock our group facilitator, a plump, pretty woman, about forty, introduced herself as Marian and the session began.

First Marian said we would circle the room for each woman to give her name and mention why she had come. My cheeks warmed. Because I've got this hunger in me, I thought. I've spent my entire adult life surrounded by males, my husband, my three stepsons, my own two sons, and now I want — I need — I long to be close to another woman, not just as a friend. I have lots of friends, all the friends I can use, but I want something more, a woman I can be physically as well as emotionally close to, someone I will feel excited just thinking about when I wake in the morning, someone I can hold and kiss, with whom I can talk and dream.

"My name's Jane," I said when it was my turn. "And I'm here because I used to go to the L.A. Gay Center but that's quite a distance, so I phoned there today and was told about this center, which is much closer to where I live. So, here I am."

I smiled rather tensely, bowing my head toward the young woman to my left, hoping that no one would notice that I hadn't been overly specific in detailing my reasons for attending lesbian rap sessions. I hadn't said: *I'm here because I'm gay and want to meet other gay women.* Nor had I said: *I'm here because I'm lonely and hurting and want to find that one special person to stop the ache.* No other woman had said that either, but wasn't that in truth why all of us were here, looking for love?

After we'd circled the room introducing ourselves, Marian suggested that we go around again, this time each of us relating the nicest thing that had happened to her during the week. This seemed to be the "in" thing to do in rap sessions, judging from the other ones I had attended. In the NOW consciousness-raising group I'd belonged to, we'd started each meeting by going around the room intellectually stroking ourselves, and we'd done much the same thing in the Science of Mind Church class I'd attended.

But I didn't feel any need for such stroking. I already felt good about myself; in fact, I felt great about myself. What I didn't feel so good about was my spectacular lack of success in meeting a woman with whom I could share emotional and physical intimacy. And I couldn't see that attending this meeting tonight, as excited and hopeful as I'd felt driving down here, was going to do one damn thing toward solving my problem.

When it was my turn to let everyone in on the nicest experience I'd had of late, I said, "Well, there's this extraordinarily pretty blond woman in a yoga class I take. Today was the second class, and after class I managed to walk with her down to where our cars were parked, which I thoroughly enjoyed. But unfortunately another woman was with us, so the conversation stayed very impersonal.

That said, I again nodded to the young woman to my left, smiling at her. Stroke, stroke, stoke, your turn now. But surely no one could reach any kind of joyful climax before a room full of people like this.

Once this memory-masturbation was out of the way, Marian read from a list of possible rap topics and one was chosen: how we deal with anger. During the general discussion that followed, to which I contributed nothing at all, it came out that over half the women in the room were mothers, even some of those who looked barely more than children themselves, and the most frequently strummed note was regret and sorrow over the mean, hateful, rotten cracks hurled in the heat of anger at their kids.

Sitting silently on my stool in the corner, carefully listening, I tried to think of something to contribute to the discussion but failed. Thinking back over my life from the perspective of fifty years, I could not remember a single time I had said anything in the heat of anger that I later regretted saying. For one thing, I rarely get angry. When I do, I tend to be rather detached from it; part of me stands off and scoffs. I remembered the last time I had gotten angry at my younger son. I'd felt he needed correcting, so I'd stood in front of him, while he sat looking tense and upset, his face paling, and really gave it to him, while inside me a little voice kept saying, in amusement: *Now just watch the old bag really telling this poor kid off!* But my son's behavior had bothered me and I'd wanted to prevent any recurrence. When I'd finished, Tommy lifted his eyes to meet mine and muttered, "You're right. I apologize. I promise it won't happen again." End of tongue lashing, end of anger, end of mocking voice in my head. Afterward I certainly hadn't regretted a single word I'd said.

During fights with Russ, well, I often got plenty angry then, but still with detachment. To begin with, during our early years together, when he'd blow up over something, which he did with great frequency and force, I'd simply walk away from his anger, leaving the room. Later I'd stuck around physically but emotionally had shut him out, answering calmly to turn off his wrath. In time, however, I'd learned that the soft answer doesn't always or necessarily turneth away wrath. With Russ it was more like pouring oil on a fire: he'd simply become even more inflamed. We'd been married about ten years before I realized that what he wanted from me when he was angry was for me to fight back, to match him yell for yell, decibel for decibel. So I began doing that, but inside I was still detached. I knew exactly what I was doing, calming down my crazy husband, and I couldn't remember ever saying a single thing I later regretted. How to deal with anger, either my own or someone else's, was no longer any kind of problem to me. My problem was the deep ache I felt inside, which being here tonight wasn't helping at all.

As the rap session broke up, I slid off my stool and wound my way out of the room, murmuring occasional good-nights to the women I passed, sure that I would never return. Whatever I was looking for I wouldn't find here.

In spite of my initial disappointment, I returned the following Monday night, and the week after that, and the week after that; for the next few months I rarely skipped going. One night when Marian asked for suggestions as to what we might rap about, I asked if we could discuss open relationships. Did they work? What was the experience of the other women? Everything I'd read had led me to the conclusion that once a relationship is opened up, that's it, it will soon break up. Was that the group's experience, too?

"Hey, that's a good idea!" Marian answered brightly, eyes dancing. "Open relationships. Can you open up a primary relationship without weakening or destroying it? Does anyone object to rapping about that?"

"What's an open relationship?" a young woman asked, her broad face sullen.

Marian answered, with perfect teacher aplomb, "An open relationship is one in which you have one primary relationship but each partner is also allowed other, secondary relationships. A relationship in which sexual fidelity is not asked for or expected. In other words, a non-monogamous relationship."

"What's monogamous?" someone asked, pronouncing the word with great difficulty.

"One on one" — thrown in.

"Any girl of mine, if she goes to bed with someone else, that's it, her and me are through!" the young woman to my left said firmly, which drew *amens* and *you said its* from all around the room.

Two hours later the verdict was in, affirming what had been said from the start. Open relationships were impossible, they didn't last. Who could cope? To open up a relationship was to kiss it good-bye.

A slender woman named Claire, fortyish, a junior-college teacher, summed it up judiciously: "In all my years I've yet to see an open relationship, whether in the straight or gay world, that held together. One or the other will soon fall for someone other than the primary partner and call it off. Or else, after a period of experimentation, the two will wise up and agree to close up their relationship again, usually even tighter than it was before.

"The idea sounds great: 'I love you and don't want my love to be a cage holding you in: fly away temporarily to anyone you wish, enjoy yourself, etcetera.' Or, 'You're a flower I don't have it in my power to open up completely, so I'll open you up as much as I can, then you can go to others so they can open up other aspects of you, and I'll do the same — I'll go to others, who will open me up — and that way, when we come together again, each of us can experience someone to love who is fully open, fully beautiful, etcetera.' That sounds great, sounds ideal, but in practice it simply doesn't work. When two primary partners stop being faithful to each other, or stop expecting fidelity from each other, pretty soon there's no primary relationship to worry about anymore. Apparently that's human nature, so why try to fight it? Period."

I sighed, but in spite of this summing up, which I was ready to accept and believe, in my heart I felt more determined than ever. The ache inside was stronger than fear. One way or another I was going to open up my marriage and become lovers with a woman, even if it cost me my marriage.

Following the rap session, a group of us went to a nearby gay bar where there was a jukebox and a small dance floor. Russ doesn't dance, so it had been years since I had; but in my younger days there was nothing I'd enjoyed more than dancing. The beat of the music got to me and as I watched a few couples moving onto the floor, my itchy feet took command and I glanced around the table to see whom I dared ask.

Across from me sat several younger women, two of whom I thought were very attractive, but the moment I thought this it occurred to me that if I intended to ask anyone, I should ask Frances, who sat beside me. She was close to my age. I'd seen her repeatedly at the raps and it would be an unpleasant slight if I passed her over to ask anyone else. Also, it was safer to ask her because my ego would stay completely intact regardless of how she answered. If she coldly rejected my advance, fine, I certainly wouldn't care.

"Dance, Frances?" I suggested, turning to face her.

In an instant she had bounded up, the corners of her mouth, habitually drawn down in a sullen frown, swinging up. "Hey, let's go!" She began trucking her way to the floor, snapping her fingers as she swung her hips, her loose black pants swaying around her ankles. Laughing, I followed her onto the floor.

It was fast rock music. Although Frances seemed old enough to remember old-fashioned contact jitterbugging, which was the rage when I had last danced, she didn't want to dance that way, so we made out the best we could, doing an imitation of the way youngsters dance today, facing each other but each of us doing her own thing. Frances, a skinny little thing with dark grayish skin, kept grinning and winking at me, which was totally out of keeping with the moody, miserable, misanthropic personality she had projected during the raps. She hadn't had time to gulp down much beer but she seemed to be feeling gloriously high nonetheless. I couldn't help laughing and feeling warmly fond of her.

We danced on and off for the next hour, Frances gulping down beer between dances while I sipped my orange juice. As it got on toward midnight I turned to tell her, feeling suddenly very jumpy about the time, that I just had to leave, but I'd barely opened my mouth when she bounced up to say, her thin little face twisting, that she was going to the ladies' room.

Her hand gripped my shoulder hard as she leaned down close, blasting beer fumes into my face, to order, "Now don't sneak off while I'm gone, hear? You be here when I get back, hear?" With that she turned and strode unsteadily off.

A woman sitting across from me, Ruth, winked and grinned. I smiled back. "Want to dance?" Ruth asked, but I shook my head and said I had to be leaving, I was just waiting long enough to say good-night to Frances.

Would Russ be terribly worried that I wasn't home yet? The time had flown by so quickly that I hadn't realized how late it was. I glanced around, hoping to spot a phone, but phoning was probably a poor idea anyway. Russ might be asleep already.

Guilt clamped down on me, and even though it wasn't quite midnight yet, I changed from a middle-aged fairy princess, enjoying a gay outing with all these lovely gay companions, into a harried wife and mother who had no business not being safely home in her bed.

Frances came hurrying back unsteadily, head thrust forward, hands out as though to guard herself against invisible threats on either side. Reaching our table, she plunked down, opened her purse, and pushed a pen and piece of paper toward me. "Give me your name and telephone number," she said. "I'll call you sometime and we'll get together for a friendly drink or dinner, okay?"

"All right." I dutifully wrote down my full name and phone number. As I handed the paper back to Frances I caught her eye. "But don't be upset," I warned her, "if a male answers. Just ask for me. I live with my husband and younger son."

"You *what?*" — a horrified screech.

Blushing, I repeated what I'd said.

"You're married? You mean to a *man?* Is he gay too?"

My cheeks burning, I shook my head. "No, he's straight. At least as far as I know he is."

To my embarrassment, I realized that silence had fallen upon the table. All the women seemed to be listening, with varying degrees of breathlessness, to the quizzing I was getting.

"So, does he know about you?" Frances demanded, staring at me with something akin to fear and loathing.

Know what about me? I almost asked, but decided that this was no time for sophistry. I had used up the best part of this woman's evening, passing myself off as both gay and available, and surely I owed it to her to take her indignation seriously.

"He knows where I am tonight," I answered calmly, "that I came down to attend a lesbian rap session."

— 18 —

This was true. The first few times I'd driven down to the Gay Center I'd lied to Russ, telling him I was going to a NOW meeting; but one night before leaving the house, disgusted with myself for senseless prevarication, I'd told him about the center and since then had always told him the truth when I left to attend a rap session there.

"So he knows you're gay?" Ruth asked me excitedly from across the table.

I was beginning to weary of being quizzed; at the same time, I felt closer to these, my gay sisters, than I'd felt at any time before. Tired of quibbling, I nodded in acknowledgment.

"And your son," Ruth pursued diligently, her round, Bette Davis eyes popping with curiosity, "does he know too?"

Sighing, I said, "Yes, he knows. That is, he thinks of me as bisexual; after all, he's seen me living happily with his father all these years."

Tommy not only knew, he made constant good-natured cracks about his perverted mother and her bull-dyke friends; no matter that the friends he meant, Pat and Leslie, both very feminine in manner and appearance, didn't exactly fit that description.

"Well, obviously you *are* bisexual." Ruth chortled happily, as though this made everything all right; I was now conveniently slotted away in the right pigeonhole. A.C./D.C.—no matter that, in spite of my best efforts, I had not yet gotten plugged into the D.C.

"Here's your telephone number back," Frances spat out, slapping the piece of paper back into my hand, hard. "I don't dig married women." She pushed back her chair, stood up, and wobbled unsteadily over to the bar.

Ruth slid around to the chair vacated by Frances and leaned forward toward me. Eyes glittering, she said, "Does your husband dig watching you and your girl friend together? Is that his bag?"

Appalled, I said, "I don't have a girl friend, though I'm looking for one."

"When you find one, does your husband hope to watch you and her together?"

"That may be his hope," I said coldly, inwardly trembling, though I didn't for a moment really believe this. "But it's certainly not going to happen."

"Oh," Ruth said, leaning back. "A lot of men really dig that. Boy, the number of men who've asked me if I'll make it with their wives while they watch, you wouldn't believe it. You're lucky you've got a husband who's so understanding and doesn't mind your playing around on the side."

"Yes," I agreed. Playing around? Something I hadn't managed to do much of up to now. "Well, I've really got to be going." I stood up to leave.

Claire, the slender, attractive, junior-college teacher, stepped over to stop me.

"Good luck," she murmured softly, offering her hand. She had a long, rather worried-looking face, short, graying hair, and a lovely, warm smile. "I was married too, until two years ago," she confided. "But after our youngest child left home we split up. Since then I've come out, and in spite of the bumps and bruises along the way, I really find that I'm happier." She smiled again as we shook hands. "So I wish you the best."

"Thanks." On impulse I added, "On Tuesday I have my first luncheon date with a woman I met a couple of months ago, in a yoga class, a darling blond woman I really dig, but—"

"But you're afraid she's straight?"

Sighing, I said, "Thirty years married, what else?"

We laughed ruefully together, then, clutching my purse more securely, I turned and left.

Two

We sat across from each other at a small, shining, square table for two on the patio of a Mexican restaurant, a three-tiered fountain gurgling a few feet away. Dark-skinned, shyly smiling waitresses scurried across the stone floor in brightly colored short skirts worn over thick, starched petticoats. As we waited for our menus to be brought, I dared look directly across at my beautiful, blond companion.

Amy, noticing, immediately smiled back, tilting her head. Like two idiots, we sat grinning at each other while my cheeks warmed and I began feeling even more keyed up, even more excited. The previous week Amy had mentioned that she was almost fifty-one, which I could hardly believe. How thoroughly it delighted me. She was so entrancingly pretty, looked so much like an exquisite Dresden doll, that I had half feared, even knowing that she was a grandmother four times over, that she might be as young as thirty-five. To be told that she was, instead, a few months older than I had made it seem almost possible —

Well, impossible of course — any woman who looked and dressed and smiled and spoke as she did, but still . . . Was there, by any chance, the slightest possibility?

Of course not! I warned myself. I'd told my friend Pat about meeting Amy in yoga class — that this extraordinarily pretty blonde had smiled repeatedly at me, why I didn't know — and Pat had laughed happily for me, then had gone on to remind me what a fool I'd made of myself with Vera.

"Watch it, kiddo," she'd warned. "Don't try to storm the Bastille overnight. Settle for what you can get, all right? A nice warm friendship, what's wrong with that? For God's sake, Jane, don't send another poor respectable conventional married woman into shock!"

Sighing as I glanced over at the water splashing down the fountain, I told myself that of course Pat was right. I'd known Amy for about three months. In the yoga class in which we'd met, I'd always put my exercise mat down next to hers so we could talk together before instruction began; after class we'd walk together out to our cars. I knew the bare facts of her life: thirty-some years married to the same man, whom she always referred to as "sweet and dear," two grown children, both married, four grandchildren. Her husband, in poor health, had already retired; they lived a quiet life together, Amy said, rarely going anywhere. Everything indicated that she was contentedly jogging along with her chosen mate, her life-long companion, into the twilight years without the least degree of regret or bitterness. And absolutely nothing indicated that she would have the least interest in responding to any advances from aching, hungry me!

I glanced back toward Amy again and again she smiled, again slightly tilting her head.

"She's the absolute, quintessential flirt!" I had complained once to Pat in ever-growing frustration. "Smiles on cue, tilts her head on cue, bats her lashes on cue. Goddammit anyway!"

Pat laughed. "And like one of Pavlov's dogs, you automatically salivate. Poor old Jane."

"Poor sick Jane," I muttered. "Why can't I find a gay woman I like instead of batting my head against one stone wall after another?"

"I see you're following the same ingrained pattern," Leslie had remarked cuttingly when I told her about Amy. "Setting yourself up for another rejection, as you did with Vera. When are you going to face it, Jane? You don't want to find a female lover, what you seek is rejection. Sounds like you're all set to get what you want, again."

"You're looking extraordinarily pretty today," I said to Amy across our polished little table.

I was immediately rewarded by an even more blinding smile, twin dimples spearing into her cheeks as she batted her lashes at me. "Thank you," she said, every inch the flirtatious little girl.

A waitress stepped up and handed us each a menu. Sighing, I turned my attention to mine. A moment later, pulse skipping excitedly, I noticed that Amy had opened her purse. She drew out glasses and slid them on. It was the first time I'd seen her in glasses and the sight made me feel instantly, inordinately happy. I had worn glasses since childhood, as did all the women in my family, and I had always felt drawn toward glasses wearers. Looking across the table, I found that I especially liked them on Amy. Somehow they aged and subdued her face, made her look more like a lovely mature woman instead of a bright, childlike, golden doll. Seeing her with those large, round, pale-rimmed glasses on made me instantly hope that maybe, oh maybe, she had the same human needs as mine, and might just possibly respond to me.

Catching me looking at her, Amy wrinkled her nose with a little frown, as though in apology for the human imperfection that forced her to wear glasses. "I think I'll order the combination plate," she said.

"Sounds good," I said, completely indifferent at that moment to what I ate. "I will too."

Amy hastily drew her glasses back off, folded them, and slid them back into their case and into her purse. We closed our menus and laid them aside. Glancing across at me, Amy again smiled, slightly tilting her head.

Soft blond hair, wavy around her head; a lovely, smooth forehead; deep blue eyes; a nice, undistinguished nose; deep twin dimples when she smiled; soft, unwrinkled, glowing skin; a perfectly formed mouth, which broke into brilliant smiles over even, white teeth — this was the Amy I sat across from and hungrily eyed. A lovely white throat, full breasts, a shapely waist, trimly curved hips, nice legs, a head-high, watch-out-for-me walk — my God, I just couldn't believe that a woman of fifty could look like that! When she flashed me her bright, sweet smile she looked about twelve, but a flirtatious, why-don't-we-get-it-on-together twelve. By now, after three months of this, I was in such a state of confusion and frustration that I no longer was sure of anything.

"Amy, you're beautiful," I said to her. "And you look so impossibly young."

Amy laughed. "Because I work so hard at it. If you saw me when I get up in the morning, you'd say, 'Hey, where's Amy?' 'Here I am, right here.' 'Oh no, no, not you, old lady, I'm looking for Amy, the young and beautiful Amy.' 'But that's me, *I'm* Amy!' 'Oh, sure, sure you are!' "

As Amy dropped her dialogue, her mimicry, we both burst out laughing.

Amy told me that her hair, though naturally blond, was getting gray, so she dyed it. She spent an hour or more putting on make-up before she ever ventured out. "To leave the house at a quarter to twelve today," she explained, "I had to settle down in front of my magnifying glass and start getting ready before eleven. Is it any wonder that the first time you asked me to lunch I told you I just couldn't make it?"

"Well, I'm glad you made it today," I said, feeling uncomfortably warm all over.

"I am too," Amy said, batting her lashes.

Inwardly I sighed again. Long before the feminist movement had been officially born, I'd been one; throughout my fifty years I'd had little or no truck with feminine gender reinforcements. I'd never in my life worn mascara or eyeshadow or nail polish. As a young woman I'd worn lipstick most of the time, though for a two-year period when I was twenty-one I'd forsworn even that. Back in those days, however, in the late '40s and early '50s, I'd been made to feel somewhat freakish for going about my business barelipped, so in time I'd caved in under the pressure and worn it again for a few years, on social or business occasions. At home I'd never bothered with it, in time had dropped it altogether, and hadn't puckered up my lips to apply color to them in at least fifteen years. Face powder I'd tried maybe two or three times when I was young, hadn't liked the look of it, and hadn't worn it since. Though I did customarily go to a local beauty shop for a haircut every three to four months, I'd had my hair set and waved by a beautician only once in my life, prior to a wedding half a lifetime before; I hadn't liked the result and hadn't had my hair done professionally since. Nor did I set it myself; I washed it, let it dry by itself, and brushed and combed it, period. Fortunately, it had sufficient natural wave that I felt it did fine without further care.

"You're the one who's really beautiful," Amy said suddenly, looking across at me with an earnest expression, unsmiling. "My looks come out of bottles and jars, while your beauty is natural."

"Sure it is," I said, and we grinned companionably again.

Over our combination plates—tacos, enchiladas, rice, and beans (all meatless)—I mentioned my young friend Leslie. "She and her husband agreed before getting married that they'd have an open marriage," I said.

"Oh, what's that?" Amy asked.

"Oh, you know, that while the marital bond is the primary relationship each is free to do as he wishes on the side."

"That's the kind of marriage I have too," Amy responded casually, her eyes down as she slid her fork into her rice. "Bob has never been the least bit jealous or possessive. Whenever I tell him I'm going out, all he says is, 'Have a good time, honey,' and when I return he'll say, 'Hope you had a good time,' but never a word about where have I been, what have I been doing, nothing like that. We're both Geminis and have to feel free. I couldn't live with a man who wouldn't let me be free."

My pulse skipping, I said, holding down laughter, "And does that freedom extend to the sexual area? Are you free to have all the love affairs you want?" Somehow I knew she hadn't meant that.

Amy's eyes rose quickly, and a light flush crept up her cheeks. "Oh, no, I didn't mean that. Is that what you meant? Back when Bob and I got married, well, I don't think that was done very much. If we were getting married now, the way things are today— Not that Bob ever asks me where I'm going or what I'm up to. If I said to him, 'Hey, I have this heavy date with a fellow and we'll probably go to bed,' he'd just say, 'Well, have a good time, honey.' " Mimicking voices again, she broke out laughing.

"Meaning he wouldn't even hear what you said." I laughed too.

Amy shrugged. "After thirty-two years, who listens anymore? When I got back home and he said, 'So did you have a good time, honey?' I could say, 'Oh, we sure did, we went out and rented a motel room and spent three hours there together.' He'd say, 'Well, that's nice, I'm glad you had a good time.' " After a slight pause, Amy added, "I guess it means he trusts me, which he should after all these years."

A few minutes later, undaunted by all the warnings I'd gotten from Pat and all the snide accusations from Leslie, I decided to open up, at least obliquely. Introduce the subject of homosexuality, but from a sneaky, indirect angle.

"This young friend of mine I mentioned, Leslie," I remarked as casually as I could, "the one who has the open marriage —"

"Oh, yes" — politely, attentively.

"Up to now she's confined her romances on the side to other men, but lately she's gotten it into her head that she has strong lesbian feelings too, and now she's trying to find a female partner."

"Oh," Amy said, looking directly across at me, expression unchanging. No further word, no keen look of interest, no hint of salivation, but at the same time she hadn't made a face or voiced any distaste, nor had she gone into shock. Dared I proceed further?

I picked up my taco, bit into it, wiped my mouth with my napkin, took a gulp of water, and tried to calm my suddenly racing pulse. Yes, I dared.

"She's been making a big point of it with me for several months now, over half a year. But, my God, she's only twenty-three, young enough to be my daughter. I feel very maternally fond of her, but nothing stronger than that."

Amy eyed me curiously. "You mean she's trying to get you to — become lovers with her?"

My cheeks burning, I shrugged. "Well, off and on she's tried to talk me into it, but I honestly think she's mainly just talk. I honestly think if I said, 'Okay, you've talked me into it, let's go,' she'd swing around and run like hell the other way."

"You think so?" Amy's cheeks were flushed now too. Her eyes held mine.

"Yes, I think so."

For a few minutes I let the conversational ball just lie there, too scared to carry it further.

When I spoke next, I switched the topic, mentioning another friend of mine who was in despair because a planned marriage had fallen through. "She was widowed about three years ago and doesn't like being alone. She thought she'd found a new love, was so happy about it, but then a month before they were due to get married, he pulled stakes and fled. Now she's really in the pits about it."

"Just because the fellow didn't marry her?" Amy responded, unsmiling. Her eyes met mine again. "Doesn't she realize that may be the luckiest thing that ever happened to her? If she's our age, as you say, and her children are grown and she's financially set, what does she need a man for anyway?" Suddenly Amy shuddered slightly. "My husband's a dear, sweet man, and we've been married so long now that I'd never think of leaving him, but if anything happened to him, the last thing I would do is marry again. Ugh! I'd rather go on welfare than ever marry again."

We sat looking straight across at each other for what seemed a very long time.

After we'd finished eating, we sat and talked for close to an hour at our little table, then decided it was time to leave. On the sidewalk outside, I asked Amy if she still had some time, which she did.

There was a small park a few blocks away, so we decided to go there. We drove over in my car and sat on the grass under a tree and talked some more.

"About this young friend of yours, what did you say her name was, the one with the open marriage?"

Of her own accord Amy had reintroduced the subject! "Leslie," I said.

"Oh, yes." Again Amy's cheeks were slightly flushed. "You say she's been trying to get you to become lovers for almost a year?"

"For about half a year," I corrected. "But I don't really think she means it. I think she just figures I'm safe, a way to relieve some tensions without being forced to put up or shut up." I took a deep breath and plunged in deeper, staring down at my fingers playing around with the grass, plucking blades out and curling them around and around. "But during these past few months, ever since I first went down to the Gay Center in Garden Grove—"

"Went where?" Amy asked, leaning closer, frowning intently, as though she really hadn't heard but keenly wanted to.

"The Gay Center down in Garden Grove," I repeated more distinctly. "This friend of mine, Pat—well, she's married now but she has a past history of living in the gay world, and she and I and Leslie—well, a few times we've driven down on Friday or Saturday nights to go to a gay bar near the center, where we dance and drink—except I don't drink, especially when I'm driving. But Pat and Leslie have their beer and wine and I have my orange juice, and we've made a few friends down there by now and enjoy ourselves."

"And does your husband know?" Amy asked, eyes intently on me, head slightly tilted again but not flirtatiously, tilted as though to get a better grip on the words cautiously dripping out of me.

"Oh, yes, he knows. I used to lie and tell him I was going to NOW meetings, but then I got disgusted with myself and told him the truth."

"And he doesn't mind?"

"If he does he hasn't said so." Suddenly I grinned, facing Amy directly. "Four years ago, when I first told him I was going to join NOW, he said great, he'd always liked lesbians." I laughed softly and Amy joined in.

"And that was definitely in my mind when I joined," I confessed, "but our chapter is made up almost entirely of married women. If there are any lesbians among us, they are most certainly still in the closet. As a young woman I flirted with the gay world too," I suddenly threw in.

"You did?" Amy sounded startled, drawing back slightly, but—did she look upset? Dammit, was I risking

— 29 —

losing her friendship by going so far? But how did you ever make gains if you never dared to take risks?

"I considered myself a lesbian," I said. "Well, for a time I did anyway." How busily I was plucking grass blades, wrapping them around my fingers, unwrapping them, discarding them, plucking new! "That is, by the time I was seventeen I had decided that I couldn't possibly be heterosexual. From the time I started dating—and back then every girl was expected to date, so I felt like a real freak when I didn't—but I simply couldn't handle it. I felt constricted, bound in. I hated all that role playing, though that isn't what we called it then. More than anything else, I couldn't cope with physical closeness; I felt assaulted, invaded."

I glanced up at Amy again, cheeks burning, and grinned. Amy grinned back, and we both laughed softly. What a beautiful, glowing doll she was!

"So how did you happen to get married?" Amy prodded a moment later.

"I knew I wanted a baby, I needed and wanted someone to love, and I couldn't seem to manage with either men or women—I couldn't handle the physical side, making love. But by the time I was twenty-six I wanted a baby more than anything else, so I forced myself to plunge in. How about you," I asked, "did you want children too?"

"Oh, yes," Amy said, her face softening into the sweetest smile. "From the time I was seven, playing with dolls, I wanted more than anything to grow up and become a mommy. That's the nicest word there is, I think, and *grandma* is second."

"You're nice," I said, "and so damn pretty."

"You're the one who's really pretty," Amy said.

All too soon it was three o'clock and I knew I had to be getting home. I drove Amy back to her car at the restaurant parking lot, walked with her to it, and stood alongside it to say good-bye.

"How about lunch again next week?" I asked.

"Which day?"

"I don't care, whatever day's convenient for you."

Amy frowned. She fooled with the sun shield in her car, bit her lip, then glanced around and smiled rather hesitantly. "Well, let's just play it by ear, all right? I'm not sure this minute when I can make it. Call me, okay?"

My heart sank. "All right, I will." I stood there and we continued to look steadily at each other.

"I do love you," Amy said suddenly, softly, as though just at the moment deciding she did.

"And I love you." Heart pounding, I leaned forward into the car, but very slowly, giving her ample time to turn her face away, as I expected her to, but she didn't. Instead, she puckered her lips just slightly and I found myself, in surprise, kissing her not on the cheek but on the mouth.

"Thanks for the lunch." Smiling, she started her car and backed it around to leave. I watched, sighing. She threw me one last little wave, then her car was dipping down the incline to the street. She turned to the right and sped out of sight.

I do love you, she'd said, but she'd also refused to make another luncheon date. Dammit, I thought, have I goofed up again?

That Friday night Pat, Leslie, and I went down to the gay bar near the center. My luncheon date with Amy had been on Tuesday. On Thursday morning I'd phoned her, pulse racing, asking if she'd have lunch with me again on Friday. After all, she'd told me she loved me.

"Oh, I can't. Sorry, but I'm busy."

"How about next Tuesday, then?"

"Well—well, I don't know, Jane. Can't we just play it by ear? I'll see you next Monday in class and we can decide then, all right?"

"All right"—heart sinking fast. We talked a bit longer but the conversation limped awkwardly, and before long I felt obliged to hang up. Had she seemed rather cool, less friendly than before? Having had time to think over all I'd said, was she now retreating?

Feeling restless and gloomy Friday morning, I had phoned Pat, to find her zippy and cheerful. "Let's go somewhere tonight," Pat had suggested. Her husband was leaving on a fishing weekend, so she wanted to go out and raise a bit of hell.

I stalled around a minute or two, then agreed. "I'll phone Leslie and ask if she wants to go too."

Leslie drove over to my house, then together, in my car, we continued on to pick up Pat. I was full of thoughts of Amy, of our Tuesday luncheon date, but reluctant to discuss it. Feeling sick that I'd probably already blown it, the last thing I needed was more *I told you sos* from my friends. Why hadn't I paid more attention to their play-it-cool, play-it-smart suggestions? Was I ever going to learn not to be so open and direct?

"So how are things going with that pretty blonde in your yoga class?" Pat asked me almost as soon as she climbed into the car.

"What pretty blonde?" Leslie leaped in, apparently forgetting the conversation we'd had.

Pulse racing, I said, "Oh, a woman in the class, about my age, name's Amy. Very pretty, very married. I told you about her."

"Oh, another one of those!" Leslie said, sniffing, smiling tensely.

I burst out laughing. "Well, dear, you're married too," I reminded her. Over the months I'd known her I'd grown extraordinarily fond of her.

"Oh, not really," Leslie protested.

"And does your husband know that?" Pat inquired. "Or is it one of those cases where the husband is the last to know?"

"All right, so let's just drop it," Leslie snapped, so we did.

After we arrived at the bar and took a table, Claire came over to say hello. "I've been thinking about you off and on all week," she said, "wondering how your luncheon date with the pretty married woman came out. Did you enjoy it?"

"Oh, yes," I said, cheeks warming.

Claire eyed me, then allowed herself to ask, "But I don't suppose you had a chance to sound her out very much on your first date and all?" Her eyes lingered curiously on me.

"Well, yes, as a matter of fact I did," I admitted, feeling even warmer. "I told her about coming here and about attending the lesbian rap sessions."

"Jane, you didn't!" Pat threw in despairingly.

"Of course she did!" Leslie sneered.

"So how did she take it?" Claire asked anxiously, swinging around to sit on the empty chair beside me.

"Well," I said, face on fire, "she certainly didn't go into shock. She stayed very friendly, but at the same time she didn't clap her hands and say oh goody-goody, this is just what I've always wanted, a gay relationship. And when I asked her if we could have lunch together again next week, she said we'd have to play it by ear, she was too busy to set another date right then."

"Naturally," Leslie said.

"Too bad," Claire said sympathetically, pressing a warm hand on my arm. "Well, I'd better be getting back to my friends. See you later." With an encouraging little smile and another squeeze of my arm, she stood up and left.

"So you set yourself up for another rejection," Pat said disgustedly, shaking her head. "Dammit, Jane, when are you ever going to learn? If you want to become friends with someone, don't go blabbing your fool head off."

"I blabbed to you," I said defensively, "which worked out all right."

"So I'm different," Pat said, not cracking a smile.

"And I blabbed to Leslie."

"I'm different too," Leslie said hurriedly. "With me you knew it would work out all right, that I'd understand and be accepting."

"How did I know with either of you?"

"You just did."

I turned my eyes away, feeling sick. "So maybe I knew it was all right to be frank and open with Amy too."

"The hell you did!" Pat exploded, looking even sicker for me than I felt for myself. "You just set yourself up for another goddamn rejection is what you did!"

"Which unconsciously is just what she wants," Leslie purred. "Don't you understand that about Jane even yet?"

"Oh, hell." Grabbing my glass, I stood up quickly and walked unhappily to the bar for a refill of my orange juice.

Three

For our second date, a week after our first, I invited Amy to my home for lunch, and, to my great relief and joy, she accepted, though she asked me to promise that I'd fix something very simple, that I wouldn't go to a lot of trouble.

By then I was getting somewhat more finely tuned in to the dos and don'ts of courting her.

I'd decided during the weekend following our first lunch together that if I wanted to get anywhere with her there were two cardinal rules I'd better follow: one, not ask her to go anywhere that she might think, mistakenly, would cost her money; two, never offer to pick her up at her home but always suggest that we meet somewhere in public or at my home.

By following these two rules I'd gotten a quick and friendly yes from her when I'd tried to get her to set a date. My confessional spouting about my gay interests hadn't turned her off after all; she was ready and willing to see me again.

Not having the least idea what foods Amy liked, though I knew she was very much into health foods, I fixed potato salad—unpeeled potatoes, home-canned pickle relish—a fresh fruit and sour cream salad, and a tossed salad of greens newly picked from my husband's garden.

When Amy arrived, knocked on the screen, and called out, "Hi, I'm here," I hurried to let her in, feeling absurdly happy.

She stepped inside with her flirtatious, little-girl smile and immediately leaned forward, puckering for me to kiss her. As the kiss ended she drew back, then as we walked toward the dining area she handed me the book that she was carrying and murmured that she thought I might enjoy reading it.

The book was Catherine Ponder's *Pray and Grow Rich*.

After reading the title I looked around at Amy, saying in surprise, "Oh, do you want to be rich?"

Momentarily she looked just a trifle taken aback, then she smiled sweetly and said, "Who doesn't want to be rich?" tilting her head flirtatiously. The next moment her eyes shadowed and her smile weakened a bit as she tried to add gaily, "The fact is, I've been poor all my life and I'm sick of it."

I felt so moved I stepped close to kiss her a second time, a kiss she immediately, obligingly, puckered up to share.

That day, and almost every time I saw her thereafter, I was constantly struck anew, whenever I looked at her, at how impossibly pretty she was, her lovely, soft mouth breaking over perfectly even, gleaming white teeth.

"Well, they may look pretty good," Amy responded once when I remarked on what beautiful teeth she had, "but they aren't half as good as they look." She opened her mouth to show me various fillings, adding with a laugh that she just wished she could get her hands on the fortune in gold that was in her teeth. In such little ways I began to see, though she resolutely refused to discuss the subject with me, that money, or lack of it, was a constant preoccupation with her. But, as a determined believer in positive thinking, she fought against ever letting any negative thought or word slip through.

For our third lunch together we met again at a downtown restaurant. Everything went smoothly until the waiter brought the check, at which time Amy immediately picked it up. Taken by surprise, I reached over and grabbed it from her; she tried to grab it back, insisting that she was going to pay. "My husband and I have always paid our own way," she threw at me proudly, scowling at me. Suddenly laughing, I said this was one hell of a way for two mature, middle-aged women to act, fighting over a check in a restaurant.

"Then let me pay it," Amy murmured. "After all, you paid last time."

"And I'm also going to pay this time," I said quietly but firmly, my pulse banging. I felt we had hit a crucial moment; if I gave in and let her pay, that would be that, she would never agree to have lunch with me again. Not because she wouldn't want to see me, but because — if we were going to make it dutch treat — she would have to back out, not having the money to spend.

With a little shrug, Amy gave in. Opening her purse, she murmured, "Well, at least let me leave the tip," but I wouldn't allow that either. When the confrontation finally ended, Amy offered me her sweet, flirtatious smile and said, "Thank you," and I felt that she was pleased. Surely she knew too that if we were going to continue seeing each other, the one thing I most wanted, this was the way it had to be.

After lunch we headed over to sit in the park for a while, which became a regular thing for us. It was late spring then, the days were beautiful, and it was lovely to be outside. In addition, the downtown restaurants we went to were only a few blocks from the high school my son Tommy attended, so we'd stay in town, talking, until it was time to pick him up. After school let out for the summer we still went to the park, as, surrounded by strangers, we had more privacy than was available at home with Tommy there.

As we sat in the park following our second luncheon out, I suggested that we lunch together, again, that Friday. Amy frowned, staring down at the grass, then murmured, "Oh, Jane, no, I just don't want to." Her eyes flashed up, glinting with tears. "I can't keep taking advantage of you like this."

A sudden lump in my throat, I took hold of her hands and forced her to face me. "Amy, listen. I love you. That means that everything I have is already yours, therefore there is no possible way you could ever take advantage of me. Don't you see that?"

"I love you too," she murmured, her tears edging out, and as she leaned forward I did too, and we kissed a few times, sitting there holding hands in a public park.

As we walked toward my car a bit later, I asked Amy never to turn down any invitation I extended due to any financial consideration, and told her that I would never invite her anywhere without expecting to pay and without being fully able to pay.

Amy's eyes caught on mine. She stepped over a bit closer, put her arm around me to give me a hug, and said, "Oh, Jane, you're so sweet." I stopped walking and we kissed again.

Well, thank God that's settled! I thought, and stupidly, naïvely, I thought that it was.

During one of our early luncheon dates, Amy told me, low-voiced, making a face, that while she loved her husband, her son, and her grandsons, at the same time she couldn't stand men in general and hated being around them. She reiterated that if anything should happen to her husband she'd rather go on welfare than ever marry again; now that her husband, Bob, had thankfully lost all interest in sex, under no circumstances would she ever have anything more to do with men.

After she'd said this, I sat eyeing her thoughtfully, pulse near to bursting, then asked her, as casually as I could, "And how about a woman?"

At first she seemed not to hear—out of fear, I'd spoken very quietly—but then abruptly she took in what I'd said and grinned broadly, her face flushing. "Oh, well, that's different," she said, laughing. She had told me earlier that she had always enjoyed being physically close to women, hugging and kissing them, and that years ago she'd run across a picture of two women kissing and had so enjoyed looking at it that she'd cut it out and still had it, hidden in a bureau drawer.

I summoned all my courage and asked her if it had ever occurred to her to find one special woman and become even closer.

As she took in what I was asking, her eyes lowered—we were again in the park, sitting cross-legged on the grass, facing each other—and she began biting nervously at her lip, her face flushing more noticeably than I'd ever seen it before. Finally, as though confessing something truly shameful, she murmured, "Yes, for three or four years, I guess." Then her eyes suddenly flashed up, with an odd, beseeching look in them, a look I couldn't understand but which for some reason tore at my heart.

I reached over to take her hand, my heart pounding hard. "All the time I've been chasing down to the Gay Center looking for someone!"

Amy smiled nervously, squeezing my hand. "While I've been here all the time, only a few miles away. Why didn't you find me years ago?"

In spite of such reassurances that Amy not only understood but reciprocated my feelings for her, I lived in a constant state of anxiety, afraid that if I let it slip out in so many words—"Amy, I not only love you, I'm *in* love with you"—she'd get frightened, like a shy little deer, like the naïve twelve-year-old that she so often seemed, and run off.

I simply couldn't believe that a woman who had lived such a completely heterosexual life, falling madly in love at eighteen, marrying, having children, loving those children, loving her grandchildren, still the devoted wife of the same man—never mind that he had lost all interest in sex; Amy had mentioned that she'd never had much interest in sex, that throughout her married life she'd been frigid—how could such a woman accept a complete upheaval of her selected role, switching from A.C. to D.C. in mid-life?

No matter what Amy said, how consistently she maintained that she couldn't stand men and loved women, enjoyed being physically close to women, I still couldn't quite believe that when it got right down to the bottom line, she meant what she said. It reminded me of what I'd once read in a book on lesbians: The hostess of a party gets drunk, takes one of her female guests into her bedroom, and kisses and fondles her; then, when the lesbian partner of the young woman upon whom she's been lavishing all this attention comes looking for her and frees her from the woman's embraces, the woman, abruptly sobering up, cries out, in sudden enlightenment and total rejection: "Oh, my God, you're lesbians!"

I thought that Amy might just possibly be that kind of uncomprehending, nonanalytical woman, a woman who felt it was perfectly all right to love, kiss, hug, even fondle another woman, but, my God—the horror of it!—a *lesbian?* Never.

Late one afternoon while we were sitting in Amy's car, I told her—the most open statement I'd ever made—that I was so physically attracted to her I lived in a state of constant frustration. Amy tilted her head, looked at me with great love, and murmured, "So what can we do about it?"

Pulse racing, immediately frightened, I backed off. "Nothing," I assured her quickly. "No problem. I can handle it all right, but—well, dammit anyway, Amy, I simply can't understand you. I keep expecting you to suddenly withdraw, act frightened, or — or *something*, but you don't, which I simply can't understand!"

"Frightened of you, you mean?" Amy responded, all but laughing, her eyes twinkling. "Why, Jane, you're as gentle as a little lamb; why in the world should I be frightened of you?"

Was Amy crazy — or was I?

Here I was, doing my damnedest to draw this woman into a relationship considered perverse and degrading by the society we lived in, one proscribed by law in many states, one that, according to accepted opinion, ran contrary both to human nature and to God — and all Amy said in response to my open avowal of physical love was that I was as gentle as a little lamb and there was no reason to fear me!

Was she right?

Did she really take in what I was trying to draw her into, or was she just too simple-minded and naïve?

Though by then we were seeing each other two or three times a week for lunch, staying together for hours, talking our heads off — or, more accurately, I was talking while Amy listened — I lived with constant frustration because I couldn't really get to her, couldn't get past her defenses, couldn't get her to open up.

I talked about my childhood, then asked about hers. Frowning, she responded that she didn't like to talk about it or even think about it, which closed the door on that.

I talked about my marriage and my sons, then asked Amy to tell me about her life with Bob. Frowning, she responded that there was nothing to tell, it was just a standard marriage. I asked her if she loved him.

"Love?" Amy echoed, half smiling, eyes suddenly very sad. "What is love? It's a trap that gets you into marriage; then, once you've fallen into the trap and the babies and bills start coming, love immediately flies out the window."

"So if that's how you feel about it, why have you stayed with Bob all these years?" I asked.

Shrugging, looking thoroughly uncomfortable, Amy didn't answer at first, but after a few moments she murmured that she'd stayed because after all they were married, had children, and what else could she do?

Only one subject consistently loosened Amy's tongue and set her to talking happily and excitedly, and that was food: healthy foods versus the rotten garbage found on supermarket shelves. Until the age of forty she had suffered numerous illnesses, one hospitalization following another, so many of them she had lost count, then she had happened into a health-food store one day, had gotten into a conversation with the owner, and, as Saul was struck by enlightenment on his way to Damascus, Amy became an instant, fervent convert, rushing home to throw out all the poisonous foods cluttering up her kitchen. In one day she completely overhauled the way she ate, and then began to enjoy good health for the first time in her life. Whereas at the age of thirty-five she had looked sixty, she claimed, now, in her early fifties, she looked a glowing, vibrant, youthful thirty-five.

"It's like everything that happened to me before I was forty was not even me," Amy explained earnestly one afternoon. "All that sickness and everything, none of that was me, that was someone else. I don't ever think about it anymore, most of it I don't even remember. When I was forty and learned how to eat right, that's when life really started for me."

Once she'd been converted to what she considered the one true gospel — you are what you eat — Amy went through a period when she passionately tried to proselytize everyone she met, even strangers in stores and on the street, but nobody wanted to listen, nobody wanted to be saved.

"So in time I learned to shut up again," Amy said rather sadly, sighing. She hadn't managed to convert even her own family. Bob, grumbling that he didn't want to hear any more about her screwy ideas, kept right on eating the same old starchy, overrefined, greasy garbage—in Amy's eyes, eating himself right into the disastrously poor health that had forced him to retire at age fifty-six. Her two children, still living at home at the time of her conversion, were equally unswayed and continued right on their paths toward physical destruction, while Amy, living by the gospel, grew healthier, happier, and younger-looking every day, right before their eyes.

She had not entirely given up, however; she still constantly prodded her husband to change, to stop eating junk and start eating the life-giving foods she herself ate, but she met with little success.

"Everything his doctor tells him, every last little word, he follows like a slave," Amy told me once, then mimicked Bob: " 'Yes, Doctor, no, Doctor, and how much money would you like for that worthless piece of advice, Doctor?' " But when *she* tried to steer him gently into healthier eating habits, he'd immediately mock and ridicule her: " 'And may I please see your medical diploma, Dr. Patterson?' 'And what medical school did you graduate from, Dr. Patterson, may I ask?' " Her voice was thick with sarcasm as she mimicked him.

Even her two children mocked and ridiculed her, although somewhat more mildly. Whenever she went to visit at her daughter's home, which wasn't often, her grandchildren greeted her with cries of, "Here comes Grandma with her usual box of ugh! foods." Amy did her best not to fall off into sin even for a day, so she took along her own food when visiting among the heathen. Her son and daughter-in-law, whenever they drove down for a brief visit, did their damnedest to avoid having to eat her cooking, preferring to duck out to a fast-food chain rather than consume her salt-free, pepper-free, sugar-free, no-white-flour/white-bread diet.

"Well, you can't live other people's lives for them, I guess," Amy ended sadly, sighing, "not even your own children's." Momentarily the bright, cheerful child vanished behind this ancient but depressing wisdom.

When Amy heard how Russ, Tommy, and I eat — fruits and vegetables straight out of Russ's garden, newly picked, mostly raw — she was jumpy-eyed with admiration and said excitedly, "I knew it! The moment you walked into yoga class that first day, I knew you ate right! Your clear skin, bright eyes, the way you walked — "

"Is that why you kept smiling at me?"

Amy flushed. "Well, that and the way you did the exercises. If I did smile at you as much as you say," she ended lamely, and with a laugh I leaned forward to kiss her, bursting with love.

Amy's husband and children not only didn't share her passion for proper diet, they didn't share her excited interest in God. Reared in the Catholic Church, Amy had fallen away and become violently anti-Christian, especially anti-Catholic, the moment she married, at age eighteen. For years she'd been a very cynical atheist, she told me, and she still sneered cynically at the wealthy, bloated Catholic Church, as well as at several other denominations. But, a few years earlier, lured into the Science of Mind Church, she'd suddenly rediscovered God, or discovered a new God, and she hadn't been the same since.

"It was like the whole world changed for me. I became an entirely different person," Amy explained. "Now I meditate — pray — all the time. He seems so close. But I know I don't have to explain that to you; you of all people know what I mean." She smiled rather shyly, blushing.

Having gotten in touch with what she felt was the spiritual reality of the universe, Amy then tried to share with her husband and children her newfound wisdom and joyous new vision, but this mission met with even less success than had her previous one. If she ever dared mention to Bob her newfound beliefs and the loving God she felt so wondrously close to, he would irritably shut her off, with open ridicule, telling her that he did not want to hear another word about "that goofy nonsense."

When telling me about this—and she didn't dwell on it, she simply let a comment drop here and there—Amy always flashed out her smile as though she didn't mind the way she was treated, as though it didn't in the least hurt or anger her to be ignored, mocked, shut off.

Bursting with her newfound health, beliefs, and incredible joy, and unable to share any of it at home, Amy began developing warm, close friendships with women she met at lectures on nutrition and in meditation groups. Before we met she had five close friends, five *best* friends, two of them in their seventies. With these five women, she could discuss the things that fascinated her, she found acceptance and shared belief, and she felt happy. And, naturally for her, she expressed her happiness in frequent hugs and kisses. But, despite her close friends and their habitual hugging and kissing, there had been some little thing still missing, something more that she'd wanted; so, she'd slowly begun to dream about finding a more special friend, one with whom she could share even greater closeness. And then I came along, nursing the same inner ache, filled with the same warm dream.

On meeting me, Amy had smiled at me warmly, flirtatiously, and that's all it had taken to set me off in determined pursuit of her—and now here we were, constantly vowing our love for each other, kissing, embracing, while I spent my days in a state of continual arousal, frustration, and worry. When Amy said she loved me, did she mean the same thing that I meant when I said it to her?

She loved each of her five best friends—she'd told me so—but I was sure that she did not bed down with any of them. Was she scheduling me to be just another friend, number *six* best friend?

During this period I introduced Amy to all my close friends and family members as fast as possible, trying to integrate her into my life as thoroughly as I could. When I'd arrange for luncheon dates at which we were joined by various of my women friends, this never seemed to embarrass or upset Amy, but at the same time she'd rarely open her mouth; generally she would just smile sweetly and say not a word. The more I saw of her the more I realized that this woman was not easy to get to know, but that didn't keep me from falling ever more deeply in love with her.

Only once during those early weeks did Amy very briefly let down her guard. One Friday when we had a luncheon date, when she arrived at my house the first thing she told me was that she'd tried to call me earlier that day to cancel out.

"I got this bad news," she explained, lips beginning to tremble a little, "and I felt so upset—but then, when I couldn't reach you, I thought to myself that I shouldn't cancel. After all, today's the day I need you most."

As I drew her close to hug and kiss her, moved by her words, tears began edging out of her eyes. Sometime later, when I started to pull away, she held on to me even tighter, saying, "Let me hold you close just a minute longer, please," which caused an instant lump in my throat. I'd rarely felt so loved by her.

During our lunch, Amy, crying quietly on and off, told me about the bad news she'd gotten. It concerned one of her grandchildren. I listened with great care, trying to be as supportive as possible, doing my best to help her find comfort in letting it all come out. This seemed to work. After we'd eaten and driven over to the park, Amy remarked gratefully that she felt much better, that it had really helped her to talk it out.

"I'm glad," I said, leaning forward to kiss her.

I'd never before felt as close to her as I did that day. Her defenses had slipped away and she'd talked so freely, seemed so genuine and real, not the beaming young child with whom I'd so often had to contend. Then the very next time I saw her she did her best to spoil the whole thing.

Two days later, when we again had a luncheon date, she greeted me by saying, "Jane, I want to apologize for the way I acted the other day, telling you all that stuff and crying. I know perfectly well that nobody wants to hear about other people's troubles, and I'm sorry."

I felt stunned, as though she'd given me a lovely gift and now was rudely trying to snatch it back.

"Amy, you're very much mistaken," I protested. "I love you and want you to share your problems with me. What else are friends for if not to be of help to each other? Besides, you said you felt better after we'd talked, so why regret it now?"

"Because I know how boring it can be to listen to other people's problems," she reiterated even more firmly. Smile and the world smiles with you, cry and you cry alone—so she was going to make sure she didn't cry in my presence again, and in this fashion drive me off.

Amy remarked once that a psychological test she had taken had shown she wasn't a happy person. "But I'm cheerful," she added instantly, flashing me her smile.

Not only cheerful but resolute, the most resolutely cheerful person I'd ever known. She shared with me unstintingly her smiles and her joys, but only that one time, during the early weeks, her problems and her tears.

Though she told me repeatedly that she loved me and therefore, just as I had phrased it to her, everything she had was mine, she couldn't begin to live up to this. All I could have of her was that which she felt safe enough to offer—the bright, flirtatious, glowing child. She didn't dare let me breach her defenses to get close to the sad and troubled woman crouching behind.

Four

One Friday afternoon as Amy was leaving my house after a luncheon date, I asked her if she could possibly get away for a weekend trip; I'd pay all expenses and drive my car.

"All right," Amy answered immediately. "Bob's going away on a fishing weekend soon, so why don't we go then?"

"Great," I said, pulse racing. "Where would you like to go?"

We hashed this around for a while, and finally decided that we'd go to the mountains, Lake Arrowhead if possible. "I'll phone first thing in the morning to see about reservations," I said, Amy said fine, and we kissed good-bye.

The following morning I was able to get the reservations, but the moment I'd mailed off a check to confirm them, I began to feel guilty. Not guilty toward Amy, whom I planned — hoped — to seduce, nor guilty toward Russ, the husband I planned to betray, but guilty toward Tommy, my fifteen-year-old son. Never before in his life had I made plans to go anywhere that he was not welcome, but how could I possibly invite him along this time?

I stewed about it all morning, simply not feeling right.

By noon, no longer able to stand the guilt, I convinced myself that there was nothing wrong with inviting Tommy along. Why not? He could invite a friend too.

So I told Tommy of Amy's and my plan to go to Arrowhead and asked if he would like to invite a friend and come along.

With a startled look, Tommy laughed and said no, no way did he want to go along. "Are you sure?" I persisted. Of course he was sure. "Well, I plan to go whether you want to or not," I said firmly. "So go," he said, and my heart lifted at once, all guilt dissolved.

Tommy's answer didn't surprise me, for at fifteen he'd reached an age where he really had no desire to go anywhere with Mother anymore. It outraged him that he still had to depend on me for transportation. He was within a few months of sixteen, already had his learner's permit, and, like most boys his age, could hardly wait for his six-teenth birthday and—freedom!—his own driver's license. Meanwhile, his expression and laugh had clearly said that the last thing he wanted to do was tag along with weirdo Mother and her weirdo friend.

Tommy had first met Amy weeks before, when, fol-lowing lunch one day, I drove over to his school to pick him up, with Amy still with me. At first sight of Amy, Tommy's broad, usually friendly face began to close up. He ac-knowledged the introduction I made with only a very sullen "Hello," then threw himself onto the back seat of the car, glowering, obviously furious at me that I'd dared to have anyone with me while performing my duties as chauffeur. This made me equally furious at him, and, though Amy and I made a halfhearted attempt at conversation as I drove home, the angry, sullen presence in the back seat made en-joyable conversation impossible.

The moment we got home and went inside, Tommy announced that he'd be in his room and went storming off down the hall.

Amy made an unhappy face at me, murmuring, "Wow, he sure doesn't like me, does he?"

"But I sure do," I said quickly, stepping over to kiss her, trying to smooth it over.

When I'd first made friends with Pat and Leslie—in Tommy's eyes, my bull-dyke friends—and one or both of them would come by the house, Tommy had been very unfriendly toward them too, though not with quite the virulent hostility he showed toward Amy. When they kept coming by, however, causing no change in his life except that his "weirdo" mother occasionally went out at night with them, with the full knowledge and consent of his father, Tommy seemed to get over his dislike and in time he even became quite friendly with Leslie, who at twenty-three wasn't that much older than he was. On occasion, in fact, Leslie deliberately teased and flirted with him, and a couple of times they even got into playful wrestling matches, both of them laughing and apparently thoroughly enjoying themselves.

With Pat, Tommy never did arrive at anything even approaching friendliness, but I felt that was as much Pat's response to him as his to her. Pat, childless, often stated that she didn't like kids, never had liked them, never would like them; Tommy was just a fixture at my house that immediately made her feel rather uncomfortable, and she rarely spoke to him; therefore, it didn't surprise me that Tommy didn't exactly warm to her either. Nevertheless, he was almost unfailingly courteous.

But Tommy's growing, fairly easy acceptance of my first two openly lesbian friends didn't broaden his tolerance to the point where he could, or would, accept Amy.

I felt this showed that his intuitive awareness was in first-class working order; from the day he met Amy he apparently sensed that here was a threat to his home such as had not appeared before. This wasn't just another screwball, bull-dyke friend, this was *danger*! And his sullen, hostile reaction was a frantic call for help.

Both my sons had known for years where I stood on the homosexual issue. Just as I had made it clear from the time they began to talk that there were certain four-letter words I did not want to hear them use (which in time broke down and I began hearing them all), they also knew that I did not want to hear any kind of racial slur and that I always challenged any demeaning or belittling comments about homosexuals.

Once when Tommy was about ten he came home from school wide-eyed, having seen that day a sex education film in which it was stressed that little boys as well as little girls should not take candy from a stranger or get into a car with one. There were grown men who went after little boys to hurt them, sometimes even killing them, Tommy explained, bug-eyed.

That was true, I admitted, then began to explain that while there were some very sick homosexual men who did go after little boys, just as there were some very sick heterosexual men who went after little girls, he should understand that most homosexual men were not like that. Most homosexual men, I told him, just like most heterosexual men, were sexually controlled, decent people who posed absolutely no threat to any child.

Suddenly my husband, Russ, who was in the kitchen overhearing this, could contain himself no longer. "What the hell kind of garbage are you stuffing into that boy?" he snapped in fury. "Trying to tell him that fairies are decent people! Honest to Christ, Jane, I don't know what gets into you!"

Sitting tightly on my instantly roused anger, I repeated stubbornly, "Tommy, most homosexuals are perfectly decent people, no matter what kind of scare talk you've heard." I lifted my eyes to stare furiously at Russ. "And I tell Tommy this for one reason only—because it's the truth. Straight men are guilty of a hell of a lot more sexual crimes—rape, child molesting, you name it—than homosexual men. Just read the statistics."

"Oh, Jesus, you're sick, really sick," Russ muttered in disgust, then turned away, ending the argument.

While he'd always said that he liked lesbians, understood why women would want to be lesbians and respected them for being so, at that point in our marriage he was still wildly intolerant of homosexual men.

It was another two or three years before Russ calmly remarked one night that for some reason he no longer felt so angry at homosexual men; after all, if that was the way they wanted to live, why should he care. He still couldn't understand it, as women, in his view, were so much more beautiful, warm, and exciting.

When our elder son, Jason, entered high school and developed a very great and excited liking for one of his male teachers, it occurred to me that I had never had a straightforward talk with him about homosexual feelings, so as I was driving him to school one day I plunged in, telling him that as he went through adolescence and into adulthood he would find himself attracted to some boys and men, just as he'd meet girls and women who attracted him, and that this was perfectly natural and he mustn't allow himself to be brainwashed by our blatantly heterosexual society.

Jason listened to this latest in "mother's informative little sex talks" with the same courtesy he unfailingly showed me, making no particular comment in response, simply murmuring "Oh" politely once in a while.

When each of my sons was about two and a half years old I had explained how babies are made, pointing out to each one, as I bathed him, his genitals and how they worked, using my own body to explain the female equipment and how that worked. When each one reached the age of about eleven, I had a talk with him about masturbation, explaining that it was the natural expression of adolescent sexuality and nothing to feel in any way concerned about.

When I had this talk with Jason, for almost the only time in his life he acted embarrassed with me and angry. Lying on his bed, face to the wall, he listened in sullen silence, then suddenly lifted his head, swung his eyes around, and glaring furiously at me, yelled, "Oh yeah, that's what you think! It'll drive you crazy, that's all!"

Trying not to laugh, I said, "Oh, Jason, it will not. I don't know where you heard that, but it's not true. Masturbation most certainly won't drive you crazy; in fact, it's perfectly natural and won't hurt you in any way."

"Oh yeah, a lot you know!" Jason muttered angrily into his bedclothes, unable to face me again.

But in spite of his less than cordial acceptance of what I'd said, a couple of years later, when Jason went into adolescence, that terrible time when youngsters are supposed to get sullen, withdrawn, irritable, angry, and rejecting, Jason sailed through it with no apparent strain at all, showing the same warm friendliness toward the family he had always had before.

In due time Jason and I, with Tommy listening, had a very explicit conversation about the various birth control methods and the fact that responsible people do not cause the conception of unwanted children. Sometime after that we discussed venereal diseases. I explained that treatment should be sought immediately if any symptoms appeared. By the time Jason left for college, at age eighteen, there were few things I knew about sex that I had failed to pass on to him.

One night when Jason was home during his college years, he, Tommy, and I got into a discussion of sexual preference, and I mentioned my opinion, which both had heard before, that everyone is by nature bisexual, that it takes a great deal of unremitting conditioning to force anyone away from the natural bisexual mold.

"Mother, I completely disagree," Jason said firmly, apparently judging from his own sexual feelings.

"Stop judging everyone by your own feelings, Mother!" Tommy threw in, grinning, and we all laughed at that.

During that discussion neither of my sons would waver. So Mother was bisexual—I musn't jump to the conclusion that because I was, other people were too, or that it was a normal, natural condition. As they perceived the world, bisexuality was definitely a minority condition, like being left-handed or red-haired or seven feet tall. Because they loved me, they accepted this about me, but nevertheless they felt it wasn't the normal, natural way to be.

Jason mentioned that he knew quite a few gay people; he seems able to accept anyone's sexual persuasion, even his mother's, with no strong feelings about it. For Tommy my "peculiarities" are definitely an embarrassment. While Tommy most certainly does not want his friends to know, Jason seems not to really care. Considering the difference in their ages, this seems perfectly natural to me. While Tommy, still living at home and therefore witness to my lifestyle, knows pretty much what I'm up to with Amy, I have not made a point of telling Jason, because I am reasonably sure he has already been informed by Tommy. Just as I feel no particular need to discuss it with Jason, I think he feels no particular need to discuss it with me. I also know that, were the occasion to arise, there is no one with whom I could discuss it with greater ease than my easy-going, good-natured, elder son.

During the years when I was so insidiously sticking up for homosexuals, even assuring my sons that they were apt to discover such feelings in themselves, I wasn't at all consciously motivated by any thought that someday I might confront them with my own lesbian affair and therefore had better prepare them for it. Rather, my conscious thoughts on the subject ran along entirely different lines: Boys from perfectly "normal" homes frequently grow up homosexual; for many of them this is felt as a secret, a shame, something to be fiercely struggled against and if possible conquered; fear of confessing their "perversion" can in many cases cause a great deal of anguish. This is what I wanted to avoid for my sons.

I wanted each one to know, as he was growing up, that I accepted homosexual feelings as perfectly natural, nothing to feel alarmed about. If they grew up knowing this, then surely, if they did grow up gay, they'd find themselves far more able to accept their feelings without a lot of stress and strain, would find it far easier to come to me, possibly even to their father, to say, "Hey, guess what, I'm gay." If they grew up straight, fine, then it wouldn't matter that I had tried to open the way for acceptance of the gay.

I love my sons, want them to grow up happy and secure, to easily accept their own sexuality whatever form it takes, so I tried my best to keep all channels open at all times, not guessing that someday I'd be glad that I'd kept this one particular channel open enough that I could be accepted and understood by them.

Today both my sons, though apparently completely or predominantly heterosexual, casually accept homosexuality in others. And they accept me for what I am, though Tommy, still in high school, is definitely embarrassed at the thought of having his friends find out.

But, as I found out after meeting Amy, to accept that Mother is bisexual and to accept with friendliness the woman Mother loves are not the same thing at all. Tommy's virulent hostility toward Amy didn't die down over the first few weeks; rather, it grew worse. When we'd pick him up together at school he rarely would even mutter hello and his sullen anger over Amy's presence was so thick and self-righteous it filled the car. In the evenings, when Amy wasn't there, he'd talk about her in the most disparaging terms, calling her a giggling ninny and the stupidest woman he'd ever met.

"Mother, my respect for you has really fallen to nothing," he told me disgustedly one night, "that you could want to be friends with an empty-headed dumbbell like that. You must want to be friends just because it makes you feel so smart in comparison, and that's sick, that's really sick!" Shaking his head arrogantly in disbelief, Tommy turned away, giving me no chance to issue a rebuttal, even if I'd been quick enough to think of one, which I wasn't. At that point I was still too hung up on the guilt of my sexual feelings for Amy, and consequently was not yet able to respond to what I later realized were Tommy's calls for help.

But about three weeks of this was all I could take. The day that Tommy told me, muttering the words between clenched teeth, that I was never again to pick him up at school with Amy in the car, that he'd rather walk than get into the car with her, I got furious and ordered him to sit himself down then and there; I wanted to talk to him.

We were at the kitchen table, both of us feeling very angry, and for a few seconds I tried to get myself under control, to marshal my thoughts and know what I wanted to say before I began. But very quickly I plunged in.

"Tommy, I've had it with you. I don't care what you think about Amy, I don't want to hear you ever again say an unpleasant word about her. How in the hell do you know whether or not she's dumb? Every time you see her you hit her in the face with such hostility that there's no way she could possibly talk naturally with you around. In any case, think what you like about her, but I don't want to hear another goddamn word!"

As I stopped to catch my breath, Tommy remarked sneeringly, "So, are you finished now?"

"No, I'm *not* finished!" I snapped. "Another thing I want to point out is that Amy constitutes no threat whatsoever to your father's and my marriage. I have absolutely no intention of leaving your father or of breaking up our home. And another thing, no matter what you think, love is not something limited so that when you give it to one person you're taking it away from someone else. The fact that I love Amy is not taking one damn thing from you, nor from your father."

When I stopped again, Tommy said, his eyes flashing up angrily to meet mine, "So, are you finished now? And I really don't care who you love."

After a moment, sighing, I said, "Yes, I'm finished now," and Tommy immediately stood up and righteously sauntered off, leaving me completely unsure whether I'd accomplished anything at all.

But I soon found that I had. Apparently what I'd said had sufficiently allayed Tommy's fears, because from then on everything changed. The following Tuesday, when I told him that I had a luncheon date with Amy and that she would be with me if I came to the school to pick him up, then asked him if he still wanted me to, he said yes at once, as though anxious to wipe out the memory of his statement that he'd rather walk. For the first time, as he climbed into the car that day, he said hello to Amy with some slight degree of friendliness, and, although that's all he said, we drove home without the thick, sullen silence of earlier days. Tommy and Amy never became really close, but from that day on Tommy tried to match the wary affection that Amy had always felt toward him. He was never again openly discourteous to her, nor did he blast her verbally to me, although he certainly wasn't above taking a casual verbal swipe at her once in a while, just as he did at almost every adult he knew, including his father and me.

When I told Russ that I'd made plans to go away for a weekend with Amy, he said fine, that was great, answering in such a casual way that I couldn't tell whether he knew that my relationship with Amy was something a bit more serious than my other friendships. Feeling far too uptight at that time, I had no desire to confide in him. Besides, what did I have to confide? Up to then I'd never been unfaithful to him; all that had happened was that I fervently hoped I'd soon have the chance to be.

After telling him of the trip, I mentioned in passing that I had suggested to Tommy that he invite a friend and come along with us.

Immediately angry, Russ snapped at me, "Oh, for Christ's sake, why did you do that? What the hell's the matter with you? You don't drag along a teen-age boy when two women friends go off on a trip!"

Instantly angry myself, I snapped back that I had invited Tommy to come because I'd wanted to. I had thought it would be fun to have him along. But in any case he'd turned down the invitation, saying flatly that he didn't want to come.

"Well, good for him," Russ muttered, mollified. "At least he's got more sense than you have." End of flare-up.

The days dragged on until the night before our departure. We planned to leave fairly early Friday afternoon, which would get us to Lake Arrowhead in time for dinner Friday evening. Then we'd start back sometime Sunday, arriving home Sunday evening. I felt both excited and nervous. Only twice before had I gone away on my own on weekend trips, both times to retreats sponsored by the Science of Mind Church, which at that time I was attending. But this trip—this one was different. This time I hoped to come back a "fallen woman," an experienced lesbian.

That Thursday night Tommy suddenly asked me to come to his bedroom for a moment because he wanted to talk to me. After shutting the door, he told me in a rather low, nervous, conspiratorial whisper that he'd changed his mind and wanted to come with us after all.

I stood there stunned, unable to believe my ears.

"But—but you haven't asked anyone else. And what would you do with yourself? I mean, going with just Amy and me—"

"Oh, that's all right, I'll find plenty of things to do to keep me busy," Tommy assured me, still very nervous. He stood beside me near the door, leaning with one hand pressed on the wall, his spindly teen-age body towering over me. He'd caught me so by surprise that I could hardly think, hardly catch my breath.

"But, Tommy, when you said no—I mean, I didn't reserve a room for you, you know that, and to get one now—"

"Well, that's all right," he said quickly. "I'll just sleep on a cot in the room with you. If it's like that cabin we had when we went to the mountains before—"

When we'd gone before there'd been six of us, a friend of mine and her two children, me and my two sons, and we'd had two bedrooms with double beds, plus a pull-out double bed in the living room. I certainly hadn't arranged to have anything like that at Lake Arrowhead.

"But—oh, for God's sake, Tommy," I argued nervously, feeling sick, "I can't just spring you on Amy at the very last minute like this. I only reserved one room, with twin beds. The best I can do is try to see if I can get another room for you, which might not be possible this late."

"Well, try anyway," Tommy pleaded, still looking nervous and terribly strained.

In something akin to a state of shock, I walked out to the kitchen and called the information operator to get the number of the Lake Arrowhead lodge where I'd made the reservation for Amy and me.

Russ overheard me and came charging over to intervene. "What the hell's Tommy putting you up to now?" he demanded furiously.

Trembling, feeling more than a little sick inside, I said, "Well, he's decided he does want to come after all. I want to see if I can get him a room."

"The hell with that!" Russ exploded, grabbing the receiver from me and slamming it down. "You're not going to drag him along everywhere you go. What the hell's the matter with you, can't you ever say no to that boy?"

So what the hell's it to you whether or not I take him along? I thought irritably. At the same time, I felt a new, different guilt spring up, one that asked me whether it was true, as Russ so often insisted, that I spoiled my sons and was so gutless with them, such a thoroughgoing patsy, that I couldn't say no to them even when I knew that I should.

"If he wants to go, I'll be happy to have him along," I said as evenly as possible, again picking up the phone receiver. "I think it might be fun to have him with us," I added, gaining assurance, only half lying. Tommy's presence might even add to Amy's and my weekend together, I thought, as long as I could get him a room of his own so that he didn't wind up sleeping on a cot in our room!

"Christ, you're hopeless," Russ muttered, then gave up and walked away.

I was dialing the information operator when Tommy came striding in to say sharply, "Mother, forget it." Replacing the receiver, I swung around to face him, and noticed the pinched and angry expression on his ordinarily happy, open face. Was this last-minute, anxiety-ridden need to go based upon some intuitive awareness that only by tagging along could he save Mother from emotionally deserting him, from plunging into a love affair that would in some ways cut him out? Or, entirely characteristic of him, was it based on a last-minute, frantic fear that if he didn't go with us he would miss out on something, on some other-side-of-the-mountain fantastic fun? He'd pulled this on me a few times before, deciding at the very last minute that he wanted to go places with me after earlier refusing the mere suggestion. In each case had it been some sudden inner panic at the thought of allowing me that much freedom from him, or had it been simply a last-minute, greedy fear of missing out?

"But I don't mind in the least trying to see if I can get you a room," I told him, and by then this was the truth—I didn't mind. If he wanted to come along, I felt sure it would work out fine.

"No, no, forget it," Tommy said, his face still looking pinched and unforgiving, then he swung around to return to his room.

Sighing, I followed, knowing I'd get no further insight into either his decision to go or his reversal of this decision. In the mood he was in, with that tight-lipped look, probably all I'd get was a quick chopping down, but nevertheless, due to my own inner guilts, I felt compelled to give it one more try. I was not only not accustomed to going places without inviting him, I was not accustomed to going anywhere where, in all truth, I didn't want him to come along.

He had already shut his bedroom door, but after a quick double knock I opened it, stuck my head in, and said, "Tommy, are you sure?"

"Yeah, I'm sure." A book already propped up before his eyes, he lay stretched full length on his bed. And his voice, while not exactly friendly, was not entirely unfriendly either.

Sighing again, I started to close the door, but Tommy's voice stopped me. "But, Mother, you will give me a little money to get me through the weekend, I hope?" This time his eyes rose from the book to meet mine in hope.

"Of course," I said.

"How much?"

Tommy, unlike his elder brother Jason, had always been a thoroughgoing, dedicated materialist, had always had large, passionate wants, and, even though we gave him four times the allowance we'd given Jason at that age, he always had an impossible time getting by. Therefore, whenever I got a little something extra, like this weekend trip, he naturally hit me on the side for a little extra too.

"Oh, thirty dollars," I suggested, in my calmest, Mother-knows-best tone.

Tommy couldn't quite hide the immediate, excited gleam in his eye. "Great," he said. "Thanks."

As his mouth curved irresistibly into a pleased little smile, I closed his bedroom door behind me and walked back down the hall, telling myself that I wasn't really bribing him, and even if I was, so what? In rearing my two sons, I'd never found that there was the least thing wrong with bribes. Didn't adults, even the most mature, responsible adults, spend their entire lives bribing one another? And the thirty dollars I'd just offered Tommy was, for me, a cut-rate bargain compared to what it would have cost to take him along; his room for two nights alone would have been twice that much, plus food, entertainment, and who knows what else. I had two hundred dollars tucked away in my wallet for Amy's and my expenses, with our room already paid for. In light of that, Tommy had settled for about fifteen cents on the dollar. But he seemed very pleased, so I was pleased too, all my guilt dissolved.

How it would all have worked out had Tommy come to the mountains with us that weekend I haven't the least idea, but he never seemed to regret not having come. Any lingering hostility that he'd still felt toward Amy apparently dried up and blew away.

Five

I pulled into Amy's driveway promptly at two-thirty, as planned, very pleasantly surprised by the appearance of her home. This was the first time I'd been there, and she had always seemed so reluctant to have me come over that I'd begun to feel a little nervous about it. Certainly there was nothing about the exterior of her house to explain her self-consciousness.

A standard, suburban tract home, one of the tens of thousands hastily thrown up during the building spree of the 1950s and '60s in southern California, it appeared about the same size and in about the same price range as the house Russ and I had bought twenty years earlier and still lived in, but Amy's looked in far better repair. Newly painted a bright, pleasing yellow with sparkling white trim, it had a beautifully tended front yard, which was far more attractive than the rather straggly front yard our house boasted, and a broad, new-looking, shiningly clean cement drive, whereas the asphalt drive at our home was broken and cracked in every direction. Having seen my home, why should Amy have felt in any way uptight about my seeing hers?

I'd barely pulled into the drive when the front door opened and Amy stepped out as though she'd been standing right inside watching for me, which didn't surprise me. Apparently she didn't want to risk having to ask me inside, though whether this was due to embarrassment over home or over hubby I really didn't know. Anyway, I was far too excited to care. Grinning, I shut off the motor and climbed out quickly.

Amy, attractively dressed in blue slacks and white blouse, was carrying two suitcases, which she immediately set down on the porch, then hurriedly locked the front door. My pulse, which had been racing madly all the way to her house, now leaped even more exultantly. We were off, just the two of us, my beautiful sweet darling and I.

The door lock tested, Amy picked up her two cases and came hurrying down the porch steps, her face, like mine, flushed and smiling. "Hi," she greeted me gaily as I hurried over to take one of the cases from her, my breath catching with the remembered line, *"Come live with me [if only for the weekend] and be my love/And we will all the pleasures prove . . . "* I hope to God we do, I thought.

"Hi," I answered her. "All set?"

"All set," Amy agreed, and with broad, conspiratorial smiles we hurried to my car, stashed her bags alongside mine in the trunk, and a moment later we were climbing into my car, ready to embark on our first trip together.

Now that I was going to have her all to myself for two whole glorious nights, shut off from all prying eyes, sharing a room, I simply had to tell her exactly how I felt—that I was madly in love with her and wanted to make love to her. If I chickened out on this and settled for the same kind of warm hugs and puckered little kisses we'd shared up to now, I'd kill myself.

Of course it would be almost as bad if I got up my nerve, told Amy, and she sweetly and gently told me to sit on it, that she loved me but not *that* way.

Worst of all, by far the worst, would be if I told her how I felt, she was accepting of it, and then at the very last moment I panicked, fleeing from the terrifying threat of sexual love.

For some reason, I'd come into this life with a very deep-seated fear of sexual intimacy. It would be lovely if I could claim that in my childhood such-and-such a horrifying thing had happened to me, leaving me scarred forever after, but nothing had. No adult, male or female, had touched me with lecherous hand or otherwise laid the foundation for fear and guilt. I had never been raped, erotically fondled, or physically mistreated.

Nor had I, as far as I was aware, been given an unhealthy mental or emotional attitude toward matters sexual. Intellectually I thought sex itself was fine, normal, natural, in no way dirty or shameful. I had not the least problem with the *idea* of sex—I just had problems indulging in it.

Ever since I'd met Amy I'd been working, praying, scheming to get myself backed into the corner I was backed into now. Surely I wouldn't live to regret it!

"Hi," I said to Amy again, grinning at her and reaching for her hand. "I'm feeling so happy and excited I'm ready to burst."

"Me too," Amy said, laughing softly. Her curly blond hair blew softly in the breeze from the open car window, her eyes sparkled and her skin glowed. I ached so to be close to her, to hold her and make her mine; surely I wouldn't falter and fail. A loving God wouldn't let me, I hoped.

Just a few months before, after I'd first met Amy, I'd had a vivid and startling bad dream, one of those dreams so real that it takes minutes upon awakening before you can convince yourself that it didn't really happen.

The dream was extremely simple. I was holding a cake doughnut that had thick chocolate frosting. My two sons stood on either side of me, jeering and sneering at me. The doughnut had already had a bite taken out of it, not by me, but I now planned to eat it. As I lifted it to my mouth, however, I saw that someone had spread thick red catsup all around the doughnut, on top of the frosting. This made me pause with distaste, as I don't care for catsup on chocolate cake. After a slight hesitation, however, I decided to proceed and take a bite of the doughnut anyway—I love chocolate cake, chocolate doughnuts, anything chocolate—but as I drew the doughnut even closer to my mouth I saw that there was a hair on it. I used my fingers to pluck the hair off, still intending to take a bite, but then I saw that the catsup-smeared chocolate doughnut had hairs all over it. There was no way to pull all of them off no matter how hard I tried. Then in a panic I woke up, trembling, filled with fear and distaste. How could I ever eat a doughnut as disgusting as that?

A few nights later as I was driving down to the gay bar in Orange County with my friends Pat and Leslie, I mentioned the brief dream, telling it to them in full, glorious, nauseating detail. When I'd finished, Leslie said, rather crossly, "I don't get it," and I burst out laughing, feeling my cheeks warm.

"Oh, sure you do," I said. "Think about it."

A half minute of silence and then Leslie said again, leaning forward from the back seat, sounding even grumpier, "I still don't see the point of that dream. Sounds pointless to me."

Embarrassed, I said, "Well, for heaven's sakes, think of a hole that sheds blood—thick, red catsup—that's surrounded by hair."

"Ugh!" Leslie spat out, getting it. "What a horrible way to put it."

"And my two sons were there, making fun of me, sneering at me; since after all they are the product of heterosexual sex, in the terms of the dream they stand for my heterosexual self. In other words, what in the world do I think I'm up to—why do I think I want to find and eat such a disgusting thing as a catsup-smeared, hairy doughnut?"

"Well, if that's how you feel," Pat said rather huffily, glaring at me, "then I can't see how you can possibly call yourself a lesbian."

"Which I've never done," I said hurriedly. "I've always been keenly aware that up to this point in my life I don't really qualify. It's what I've always wanted to be, but as the dream shows, I'm too sexually repressed and frightened. But at least now I'm working on it, and the conflict is breaking through in my dreams."

Eating the doughnut—I glanced around at Amy again, smiling, and she smiled back. "Has Bob already left on his fishing trip?"

"Oh, yes. He left about noon."

"He'll be back on Sunday?"

"Sunday night. Same as we will."

She grinned and winked. I squeezed her hand, laughing. The better part of three days and two glorious nights.

Before I turned on the car motor, I opened my purse and drew out two fifty-dollar bills, handed them to Amy, and asked her please to keep them.

"But why?" she protested softly, her smile dying in a worried little frown.

"Well, in the first place," I said, "it's safer not to keep our money all in one place. If anything should happen to my purse, we'd still have that money there. But even more, well, I want you to have it, just in case you get bored with me, or angry, or whatever. I don't want you to feel dependent on me, don't want you to have to stay with me if you don't want to. All right?"

Smiling again, her eyes melting with love, Amy murmured, "Silly," but she dutifully opened her purse and tucked the money into her wallet, where it stayed for the entire weekend, and following our return she insisted I take it back.

After leaning over to kiss her, I started the car and backed out of her driveway, my pulse pounding excitedly. We were on our way, my love and I.

We arrived at Lake Arrowhead without incident, having talked all the way, checked into our room, went out for dinner, walked around, sat on the swimming beach holding hands as we talked some more, then around nine o'clock returned to our room, bolting the door, locking out the world. Smiling at Amy, holding her by the shoulders, I said, "Won't you walk into my parlor? said the spider to the fly."

Amy giggled. I kissed her. As usual, she puckered up, lips together. I tried to figure some way to make more of the kiss, to try to force her lips apart, if only slightly, but couldn't manage. I let her go and we began unpacking some of our things.

A bit later we wound up sitting together on the end of one of the beds. We hugged and kissed. Amy mentioned, as she'd told me numerous times, that she liked to hug and kiss her friends—as long as they were women, that is.

"This is nice," Amy commented after we'd kissed maybe a dozen times.

"Is this what you do with all your friends, sit with them and hug and kiss?" I said.

Amy eyed me oddly. "No, but I think it's nice. Women should make love to each other, I think."

"Great!" I began to unbutton her blouse, but got only two undone before she pulled away, jumped off the bed, and buttoned up again.

"That's enough," she said, looking scared.

"But you said women should make love to each other!" I sat on the bed, staring at her, my ears beginning to ring, my head to ache. But at least I wasn't getting angry or running away; I was sitting right there, ready to slug it out, or rather to talk it out, which apparently was the only thing about to transpire between us in that room that night.

"Well, I guess maybe I said the wrong thing," Amy said in a tight, scared little whisper. A moment later she stepped forward and gingerly sat down on the very end of the bed, about two feet from me. Her fingers nervously kneaded the bedspread, then her eyes came up to meet mine, an uneasy smile tugging at the corners of her mouth. "I guess maybe I shouldn't have agreed to come on this trip with you," she said, "if I didn't want to make love."

"Oh no," I said quickly. "I'm terribly glad we came, regardless of anything. And I didn't mean to put any pressure on you. I misunderstood what you said, that's all. You seemed to be saying it was okay to do whatever I wanted to do."

"So I guess I said the wrong thing," Amy murmured, staring down at the brown and white bedspread. We sat there like that, in silence, for a minute or two, then Amy's eyes darted up, her face breaking into a childlike smile. "But I do like hugging and kissing you."

"So do I," I said, and leaned over to kiss her closed, puckered lips, while inwardly I wilted. But had I really expected anything else?

Amy drew her legs up onto the bed and sat cross-legged. I sat cross-legged too, facing her. "The problem is what I've already told you about," she said, face shadowing as her eyes stayed focused on the spread. "I told you the very first day we had lunch together, right after you told me about Leslie and Pat and going down to the gay bar. I didn't want you to get your hopes up about me, that's why I told you. Don't you remember?"

"Told me what?" I asked, truly puzzled.

"Oh, you know," Amy said with a little shrug. "That I don't really care about sex anymore, I'm too old. If you want someone interested in sex, why don't you go after

Leslie? She seems like a very nice little girl." Amy's eyes came up, darkly shadowed, to meet mine.

"She is a very nice young woman," I said, "but I don't happen to be in love with her. I'm in love with you." The first time I'd dared to say it, and saying it had been as easy as pie. Now, how about a chocolate doughnut?

"Well, maybe you picked the wrong woman to fall in love with," Amy suggested, dropping her eyes.

"No, I didn't."

We began kissing and embracing again, and before long I said, "Oh, Amy, I'm so in love with you and dying to make love to you. Are you sure you won't let me?"

"Well, if you're sure you really want to," Amy whispered faintly. "If you won't be too disappointed . . . "

"Oh, no, never. God, I love you so much!"

We took turns showering, climbed into bed, and soon every river was crossed, there was nothing left for me to explore or do. As tense and awkward as I'd felt, I hadn't gotten either angry or frightened, for which I was very thankful. In time Amy fell asleep, but I lay awake till dawn, reliving everything that had happened, from our first real, lips-open kiss until the final, grateful, good-night peck. Oh, God, how I loved that woman!

We had a lovely day Saturday, boating, swimming, walking, talking, mostly endless talking, and when we climbed into bed that night I wasn't nervous and tense as I had been the night before; this night I felt like, and was, an experienced lesbian. After I'd made love to Amy, thoroughly enjoying it, we talked for hours. In bed in the semidarkness, her warm, soft flesh pressed close to mine, Amy opened up and talked and laughed with me as she never had before. I'd never felt so close to anyone, and it was the most wonderful night of my life.

Sunday morning, after we'd packed, I caught hold of Amy's arm and drew her to me.

After we'd kissed several times, she said, smiling, "Our honeymoon trip."

"God, yes," I replied, and kissed her again.

"But there'll be other trips," she said softly, and with that promise I let her go, picked up my suitcases, and followed her out.

We stayed near the lake until noon, had lunch, walked around for another hour, then left. On the drive home, bursting with joy and sudden ambition, I told Amy that my mind was now made up. I was going to buckle down to work, to write, and make us both rich. All my life I'd wanted to write, and for years, off and on when I had the time and was in the mood, I'd written and sold both confession and children's stories, but I'd never before felt really motivated to go for the big money.

Instead of being happy about this, Amy frowned. "But that wouldn't be fair," she murmured very softly.

"What do you mean 'fair'? That doesn't make sense."

I went on to argue that if her husband had been fiercely ambitious and had made a lot of money she would not have considered it unfair. Years before, she'd fallen in love with Bob; now she was in love with me. Ergo, why shouldn't I buckle down to make us some money?

"Well, I'll have to think about it," Amy responded thoughtfully, and for the very first time an uneasy silence fell between us.

A couple of times Amy had mentioned that Bob was very much like me, a nonmaterialist, a man who, according to her, would have been perfectly happy pitching a tent in the woods, owning nothing. While he had worked all their married life until his retirement, and had certainly fulfilled his responsibilities as husband and father, he had never been in the least ambitious, and had been content to spend his entire working life plodding along on a fairly low-level job. Amy had commented once, with a definite bitterness and scorn, that she had had to work almost all their married life in order to get some of the things she wanted. This had seemed a rerun of her childhood, when her immigrant parents had worked hard but in her view had never adequately provided for her. After one year of high school she'd dropped out in embarrassment over not having proper clothes.

"I got tired of having to wear the same dress every day, washing it out every night, and ironing it in the morning," Amy had told me. "And after my freshman year I just couldn't face going back and doing that for a whole 'nother year."

After dropping out she'd gone to work, and for the most part had worked ever since at low-paying, unskilled jobs. After marrying Bob, she had had the additional demanding jobs of running a house and rearing two children. And now here she was, after years of such labor, entering her fifties, forced to live on a pension that had seemed adequate when Bob had first retired but over the intervening years, with the galloping inflation, had shrunk to a bare subsistence level, to the point where she had to pinch every penny for them to get by. She had been working full time in a factory, for minimum wage, until being laid off just a few months before we'd met. The money from that job was now all but gone, and she was faced with having to go back to work again, if she could find another job.

"But do you think Bob pays any attention," Amy remarked after telling me this, momentarily letting down her guard, "or even gives a damn? How we get by financially is my problem; he pays no attention whatsoever. If I weren't as good with money as I am . . . Well, that's just the way life is, I guess."

She had been financially dependent upon her parents, and they had failed her; then she'd married Bob, and by her lights he too had failed her. Now I was claiming that I loved her, would always love her, and that I would settle down and provide her with the financial security that she longed for. But the moment I had made the offer, she had countered that it wouldn't be fair, she had to think about it, decide whether she could possibly allow it, which I understood. At this point in her life, bitter, bruised, full of insecurities, how could she possibly place her trust in anyone again?

After our talk about money, Amy rested her head back, closed her eyes, and soon fell asleep. As I glanced around at her, I felt bursting with love. This was my woman, my baby, my darling, my love. No matter what her fears were, or mine, somehow we'd make it through.

When we arrived back at Amy's house and took her suitcases out of the trunk, she invited me in, my first time inside her home. We went in the side door, set the suitcases down, hugged and kissed briefly, then I said I'd better be going. We were walking out to my car together when her husband rolled their old van to a stop at the curb in front. He climbed out and came ambling over to meet us, smiling. I saw that he was tall, a foot taller than Amy, and thin and bald. He had a rather square, sunburned, attractive face, and gentle grayish eyes, and I liked him on sight. After Amy had greeted him with a kiss and introduced me, he asked us whether we'd had a good time; we both agreed that we had.

A minute later I climbed into my car, and to my surprise Amy leaned in through the window to kiss me goodbye.

The depression didn't really hit until I was turning into my driveway. Following their honeymoon, two people in love get to live together. Already I missed Amy so much I felt empty and sick. As I got out my bags and walked toward the house, the front door opened and I glanced up to see Tommy standing in the doorway. He stepped forward to take the larger suitcase from me.

"Well, hi, Mother, did you have a good time?"

"Oh, sure," I said. "How was your weekend?"

"Fine."

Russ came striding over to meet me just inside the front door, his face flushed. He gave me a quick kiss and took the other suitcase from me. "Hi, honey. How was the trip? Hope you had a wonderful time."

"Thank you, I did."

Suddenly I was perilously close to tears. How depressing it all was, having to return to this same house, the same husband, the same son, after the incredible weekend I'd had. If Amy and I were married now, as surely we were, why had we already separated? How could I live till I saw her again?

"Then what are you looking so unhappy about?" Tommy asked, with a marked lack of real interest. He settled himself back in his usual chair in front of the television to watch "Wide World of Sports," his usual Sunday afternoon fare. "The trip was a bust, which it was bound to be considering the lame-brain you went with, except you don't want to admit it so you're lying instead and pretending you had a good time. Sure you did!"

"Poor baby," Russ murmured comfortingly, putting down the suitcase to draw me close. "Poor baby," he repeated, and pressed a loving kiss in my hair. Was he comforting me for the lousy time he thought I'd had, or the lousy hard reality of having to return home to him?

I never asked and he never said.

Six

Two weeks after our weekend trip, Amy told me over the phone one Tuesday afternoon that we were through, she wouldn't be seeing me anymore. She had been withdrawing steadily ever since our return, more noticeably every day, and when she refused three invitations in a row, without offering any explanation, I felt I couldn't stand it anymore.

Taking a deep breath, I said, "Amy, level with me. Am I wasting my time now? Have you decided not to see me anymore?" After asking, I couldn't breathe; my fingers wound tensely around the telephone wire. I leaned against the kitchen sink to hold myself up.

"Well—" soft, sad, then a long pause, a deep sigh, "yes, I'm afraid so. Don't hate me, Jane, please, but—you know—" softer, ever more softly, so that I had to strain to hear, "I have to feel free, I *need* to feel free. I told you that right from the start. I've always had to feel free, and—" Her voice faded away.

"And—you don't feel free with me anymore?"

Another sigh. "Please understand, and don't hate me, Jane, please."

"I could never hate you," I said, "but I — I can't believe it. I'm standing here dying. There's a poem I've always loved, by Edna St. Vincent Millay, and the last two lines — *'But that a dream can die, will be a thrust/Between my ribs forever of hot pain.'* " Hot tears were stinging my eyes; I did my best to blink them away. "Amy, I—"

"I'm so sorry, Jane, truly I am."

"But — but why? I just don't understand!"

I couldn't talk anymore, I was too choked up. I held the receiver smashed up against my ear and could hear Amy's breathing and sighs. For what seemed like forever we just held on and breathed and sighed into our receivers. Then, softly again, sounding even more like a scared child, Amy said, "So don't hate me, please, Jane, and maybe someday you'll even forgive me."

"I forgive you right now," I said, "and there's no way I could ever hate you. Right now I feel like I'm dying, but once I get over the worst of that I'll feel grateful to you more than anything else. I love you so much, you've given me so much— Well." I had to stop again; the hot tears were pressing too hard and my throat hurt too much.

"I'm grateful too," Amy said. "And — I'm sorry, Jane, truly I am, but — well, it's better to break off now, it'll surely hurt you less than if we kept on seeing each other and then I broke off later and —"

"But — why do you feel that someday you have to break off? Oh, Amy, I just don't understand! And I love you so much."

"But I have to be *free*," she said in a soft, scared whisper. "Jane, I'm sorry. And thank you for everything, for all the lunches and the gifts and our trip and everything, Thank you. And please forgive me. Good-bye."

"Good-bye," I said, and somehow managed to release my grip on the phone receiver and hang up.

Oh, God, I thought. Pressing my hands to my mouth, I

began circling the kitchen, not really thinking, just hurting, and looking for escape from hurt.

I left the kitchen and walked quickly down the hall to my bedroom, stood staring at my bed, then thought, Oh, I've got to talk to someone, I've got to tell someone! I went back to the kitchen and grabbed up the receiver to call Leslie. Somehow, I wanted to talk to her, not to Pat. Though I'd known Leslie's number by heart for the better part of a year, I completely blanked out on it.

With trembling fingers I searched through the little book in which I kept personal numbers until I found Leslie's. I dialed; it rang, over and over and over and over and over. *"But that a dream can die . . . "* Oh, God. *"Will be a thrust . . . "* Please answer, Leslie, please! *"Between my ribs forever . . . "* Maybe Pat—maybe Pat will be home, and for once, instead of being stern and critical, she'll see I need help—*"of hot pain . . . "* and will be sweet and gentle and supportive.

I plunked down the receiver, then dialed Pat's number. Ring, ring. Ring, ring. On and on, while I stood there hurting, mouth dry, throat dry, head dry, hurting. Oh, come on, Pat, for God's sake, answer! Where the hell are you when I need you? Oh, the hell with it!

I slammed down the receiver again, turned, and hurried back to the bedroom. I had talked to Russ over the phone just before I'd phoned Amy and had agreed to drive over to his office to help him this afternoon. And even though the sky had fallen in for me, I had to keep my word and go to his office.

Entering my bedroom, I angrily stripped off my clothes, threw them on the bed, went to my closet, yanked down a blue pants suit, and pulled it on.

You know—I have to be free! I kept hearing Amy whispering those words into my ear, in that soft, scared voice. *You know, you know—*

But did I know? How? Free in what way? Free of me?

Oh, goddammit, Amy. you love me and that's what being free means. The truth is what sets you free, and the truth is that you love me—and enough of this crap! In loving me, you're free. I can see it; why can't you? One word for freedom is *truth*, another is *love*. Love equals freedom equals truth, and the goddamn truth of it is that you love me, and there's no way you're going to shed me like this!

Standing in front of my vanity mirror, I pushed a brush roughly through my hair and stared at my flushed face, and, leaning close to peer into my eyes, I thought: Amy, no way are we finished; I love you, Amy. Then, sighing, I dragged the brush through my hair a few more times.

Two weeks before, when we'd returned from our weekend "honeymoon" trip, Amy's husband had gotten home unexpectedly right after we did. He'd cut his trip short because he hadn't felt well, and by that evening he was running a fever and was vomiting and had diarrhea.

"Poor fellow," Amy had told me over the phone when we'd talked the next morning. "He picked up a virus somewhere and he feels miserable. I've got him in bed right now, and thankfully he's sleeping, but we were both up most of the night. This happens every time he tries to go anywhere or do anything. He just doesn't have any resistance at all anymore; the moment he gets the least bit tired, he gets sick."

"I'm terribly sorry to hear that," I said, instantly feeling a nagging guilt. "Amy, could Bob possibly be upset over your involvement with me, the trip to the mountains?"

"Oh no, I'm sure he's not," she said quickly. "All he knows is that we've become friends, and after all, he went away himself for the weekend, so why should he care that I went away too?"

Over the next few days, with Amy housebound, caring for her sick husband, we discussed this issue repeatedly over the phone, without coming any nearer agreement on it. I argued that even very young children can sense emotional strain or withdrawal, and that experience had shown that children fared better when dealt with openly and honestly, no matter how devastating the problem. I insisted that Bob, after over thirty years of marriage to her, was sure to have sensed emotional changes in her—excitement, joy, withdrawal—and that it would probably stabilize things between them, and improve his health, if she would be more honest with him.

"Oh no," Amy would respond quickly, with just the slightest hint of fear. "He doesn't suspect a thing, and why should he? As far as he knows, you're just another new friend I've made, a very dear friend, and that's all. And his being sick like this, this virus he picked up, doesn't have one thing to do with us. He got overly tired on his trip, that's all, and of course came home sick."

After a few days the subject was dropped, for neither of us was convincing the other. I couldn't believe that Bob, who had struck me as a very sensitive man the few moments I'd talked with him, could be so obtuse as not to sense that his wife was up to something, just as Tommy had known almost from his first sight of Amy that Mother was up to something. I had tried to convince Amy that to leave Bob in a state of uncertainty, with no way of knowing what lay ahead, was an extremely cruel thing to do to him.

Amy disagreed, however, and apparently never volunteered any information, though I kept urging her to tell him that she and I loved each other, but that just as she was happily married, so was I, and neither of us had the least intention of leaving her husband.

On Friday that week we had lunch together, the first time we'd seen each other since our weekend trip. We'd barely gotten seated before Amy said, "I got your letter," tilting her head and gazing thoughtfully at me.

"I assumed you would," I said, immediately feeling uncomfortably keyed up, happy yet tense. It was the first letter I'd ever written her, but I'd felt so full of her, so close, so hungry to contact her, that I hadn't been able to restrain myself.

I had written that I loved her, missed her, thought of her all the time, and felt married to her, but, to ease the pain I was in, I had to begin feeling even more married to her; therefore, I wanted to set up common goals. During our weekend together she had mentioned that she needed new carpeting, and I thought that this could be our first common goal. I wrote that I hadn't priced carpeting for a couple of years but thought we should set twelve hundred dollars as a target figure. She had said that she planned to look for a part-time job to start making money for this; to speed things up, I would immediately start saving money too, setting a goal of six hundred dollars saved by October 1. If she didn't have the balance by then, I would save the other six hundred by December 1, so that she could have the carpeting installed by Christmas. Since Bob left all their financial affairs to Amy, he wouldn't question anything new she might acquire, so there was no problem there.

I also wrote that once the carpeting was in, I was going to start saving for a Caribbean cruise. She had told me, very early in our relationship, that she'd always wanted to take such a cruise, and in the letter I asked her to take it with me late the next spring or early summer.

Blushing as I remembered what I'd written almost word for word, I said, "So? What do you think?" I scarcely dared breathe.

Amy looked directly across at me for quite some time, unsmiling, then lowered her eyes and began biting nervously at her lip. Finally she sighed and said, "Jane, I told you I'd have to think it over. I'm just not sure. It seems so unfair."

"Oh, for God's sake," I protested, suddenly feeling frightened, "unfair to whom? When two people love each other, what the hell difference does it make who supplies the money? In all truth, there's nothing in the world I want that it takes money to get—except carpeting for you, because you want it. In all the years I've been married I've never really gotten anything material beyond the basic necessities, and I mean basic. I used to go for years without spending a penny on myself, which was all right. That's the way I wanted it. But now I certainly have the right to a few of the things I want, and Russ would be the first to admit that. When I mentioned to him once that when we have lunch together I usually pick up the check, do you know what he said? He snapped at me that I should pick it up every time. During our marriage I've worked as hard as he has, which he knows, and up to now the only thing I've gotten out of it, which was all I wanted, was for the two boys to get the things they wanted.

"All the years we've been married I've never nagged Russ for anything. For years he kept us strapped for every penny while he kept investing, first in the stock market, where he always lost, then, thank God, in real estate. So now we've got seven rental houses and some vacant land in three different states, and one of the main reasons we do is that I never put up any fight about it, I just let Russ have his own way. For years, while he was investing every spare cent we had, we made do with broken-down, ragged furniture and worn-out carpeting—worn clear through, not like yours with just a few frayed spots, but big holes where you could see through to the cement floor. I never complained because I really didn't care, and neither did Russ.

"Amy, Russ knows as well as I do that every time he bought another house, and they were almost always run-down, filthy repossessions, I was the one who cleaned and painted and did the repairs, plumbing fixtures, lighting fixtures, broken windows, everything I could do or learn to do, and I still do the cleaning and painting whenever tenants move out. This is only fair as Russ works hard too. But certainly I'm entitled to something if I want it, which Russ would be the first to admit. I handle the rentals, help him over at the office one or two days a week, can and freeze all the vegetables from his garden, and whenever I can squeeze in the time I write to make extra money. So why shouldn't I spend a little money if I want to? Who in hell is it being unfair to?"

I stopped, catching my breath, my eyes steadily fixed on Amy. She didn't say anything for quite some time, then murmured again that she needed time to think it over.

After lunch, as we were walking back to our cars—no chance to sit and relax in the park, with Bob still sick—Amy mentioned that she'd been feeling very tired all week, probably due to the stress and strain of taking care of her husband.

"You are taking vitamins, aren't you?" I asked, knowing that she believed in vitamin supplements.

Amy hesitated before shaking her head no, she wasn't.

"But shouldn't you be taking them? And Bob too?"

"Oh, I will," she said rather vaguely, glancing away. "I know you're right," she added, and the subject was dropped.

After we'd kissed good-bye and she'd driven off, I went straight to a nearby health-food store and bought their most potent multiple vitamins, B-complex vitamins, iron, and vitamin E. By then I knew Amy well enough to realize that, no matter how rigidly she tried to adhere to the gospel of proper nutrition, her own needs came last, always. Whatever Bob needed came first, then came her grandchildren's needs and the needs of her friends. Everything came ahead of whatever Amy might need for herself.

Rather than drive down to her house, I took the vitamins home and boxed them, then took the package to the post office; hopefully, she'd receive it the following day.

At noon on Saturday Amy phoned to say she'd gotten the vitamins. "Jane, you shouldn't have," she protested, but she didn't sound displeased. Then she laughed. "I've already taken one of each, and I'm sure I'll feel better in no time at all. Bob's already taken some too. Thank you, Jane."

"*De nada*. I love you, Amy."

"And I love you."

We had lunch together the following Wednesday. Afterward we window shopped along the main street of town. At a beauty shop Amy spent a long time looking into the window display, checking everything there; she even put on her glasses and bent down to read some of the labels. There was an assortment of creams, lotions, and other cosmetics, boxed as a gift, which she seemed to like. "I'll have to give that a try sometime," she said rather absently, taking off her glasses, straightening up, and flashing me her sweet smile.

After we said good-bye, I returned to the shop, bought the box of beauty aids, and had them mailed to Amy.

She phoned me on Friday, when she'd received the gift. "Why did you do that?" she demanded, sounding displeased. "It cost so much!"

"Well," I said defensively, "you said you'd like to give it a try, so I though you felt it was worth what it cost."

"But you didn't have to buy it for me!" she wailed. "If we passed a Cadillac on the street and I said it looked nice, would you rush out to buy it for me?"

"If I could," I said, trying to laugh, to lighten the mood. "Amy, the damn thing only cost forty dollars. I thought you'd like it."

"I do," she said, "but it's still too much money. And it makes me feel I'd better not say a word around you. When I said I'd like to try it someday, I wasn't hinting that you should go rushing back to buy it for me."

"Amy, I know that, I know you weren't. But don't you see? I love you so much — if I could afford it, I'd want to give you the whole world. Is that so wrong?"

There was a long silence before Amy said, "I love you too, but for yourself, not because I want you to spend money on me. Don't you see that? You make me feel so cheap and crumby, and guilty besides. Like that letter you wrote. I still don't know how I feel about that."

Another moment of silence, then I said, "Well, if it's such a big problem for you, let's just forget I ever wrote it. However you want things between us to be, that's the way they'll be."

"Except that you keep sending me gifts."

"Well, I won't send any more, if that's what you want."

Amy sighed. "I really don't know how I want things to be. After all, I do have a husband."

"I know that; I do too." I cleared my throat before daring to ask, "Amy, I don't suppose you could join me for lunch today?"

Another silence, then: "No, sorry, I can't. And I'd better say good-bye now. Thanks again for the gift, it was sweet of you."

"Sure it was." I laughed. "Amy, I'm sorry it upset you. That's the last thing I wanted to do. I love you."

"I know." I waited for what always followed — "I love you too" — but it didn't come. "Now I'd really better say good-bye," she said firmly.

Reluctantly, I said good-bye and we hung up.

I felt very depressed.

I refrained from calling Amy over the weekend, then phoned her Monday morning, and after we'd said hello, I asked how Bob was feeling.

"Oh, he's fine," she said, sounding vague and distant.

"Then could you make it for lunch today?"

"No, sorry. And we're just on our way out, so if that's all you phoned about . . . "

"Well, that, and wanting to find out how you both are. But if you're in a hurry I'll let you go."

"Thanks," Amy said, and hung up.

I called her Tuesday morning but there was no answer. I reached her early that afternoon, and when I asked if she would have lunch with me one day that week, she answered, "Oh, I don't think so." That was all—no excuse, no explanation, just, Oh, I don't think so. That's when I asked her to level with me and tell me if we were through. After a slight hesitation she admitted that she had decided we were. "I thought by now you would have caught on," she said.

End of "marriage," end of affair.

After I'd changed into my office clothes I grabbed my purse and hurried out of the house, no longer hurting quite as much. This was the goddamnedest nonsense, I told myself. Amy still loved me, and even though she had said she was through with me, and all that garbage about having to be "free," she still had never once claimed that she no longer loved me. If she didn't want me to send her gifts, all right; if she didn't want me to plan on taking any more trips together, all right. I'm a reasonable person, ready to accept such limitations. But to throw away what we had shared . . .

I backed my car out and sped off down into the street, feeling enraged. It wasn't that I couldn't understand Amy's position; sadly enough, I did understand. During the weeks we'd courted before our "honeymoon" trip she had been up-tight, upset, and frightened over only one thing. Not my open pursuit of her, my constant protestations of love, and my timid admissions that I not only loved her but was physically aroused by her. None of this ever fazed her, never once dimmed the soft, sweet radiance of her smile. But when I talked to her about my friend Joy . . .

After twenty-six years of marriage, Joy had left her husband and was filing for divorce. When I told Amy about this, I could hardly believe her reaction: her eyes flashed with fear, her mouth began to tremble, and in a frightened, tremulous voice she asked me why in the world any woman would leave her husband after that long a marriage.

I explained that after Joy's only son had left for college, she had looked at her marriage and found it empty, stifling, and meaningless. Therefore, after working up her courage, she had packed her bags and moved out. And now, giddy with pleasure and pride that she'd had the nerve to do it, she was thoroughly enjoying her new independence, happy with the new life she had staked out for herself.

After I explained this to Amy, who had met Joy, she trembled even more, and began spouting platitudes about duty, the selfish ideas people had these days about how it was all right to go around hurting others, and the fact that no one could possibly build happiness on another person's unhappiness.

"After twenty-six years, how could she bring herself to leave him?" Amy was tense and looked even more frightened. "So, she didn't love him anymore. My God, what does that have to do with anything? When two people get married, love is the first thing that flies out the window, doesn't Joy know that? I can't understand how she could have broken up her marriage after all those years."

"Better late than never, maybe?" I suggested, laughing. Then, moved by what seemed to be Amy's very real fear, I reached over, took her hand, squeezed it, and said, "Amy, relax. Many women these days are leaving their husbands, but that doesn't mean that you have to. What Joy does or doesn't do has nothing to do with you. She wanted to leave Dale. You don't want to leave Bob. It's as simple as that. No one's suggesting you break up your marriage just because Joy has broken up hers."

Because I know in my heart that, in spite of my often fiercely ambivalent feelings, I do love Russ, that I receive from our marriage not only financial support but emotional nourishment, I am not afraid to look at my marriage and consider whether or not I want it to continue. I soon learned that this was not the case with Amy.

She didn't dare really look at her marriage, for fear of what she might see. She felt that it was imperative to do one's duty, not to hurt others, and to stick by the marital agreement one has made; therefore, it was better never to look at how one's marriage was doing, for what if, horror of horrors, one spied a corpse? For the first twenty years of their marriage Bob had stood by Amy during her continual illnesses and hospitalizations; therefore, now that he was old and ill, she was absolutely duty-bound to stay with him. No other course was even thinkable.

Though no one was arguing this point with her, still Amy felt threatened, by her own inner conflicts, the ambivalence of her feelings, and the deep-seated angers and resentments she dared not face. So, better just not to look that way at all, better to keep eyes and mind shut; that way, hopefully, she'd be able to do the right thing, live up to her own expectations and see her marriage through. This approach obviously did little to enrich or better her marriage, but it kept it intact.

Then I came along, drawn to her by her underlying hungers as much as by my own, and she'd dared to risk involvement, had dared to believe that she could fall deeply and joyfully in love with me without this love becoming in any way central to her life, without our love even touching upon the other important areas of her life. But it hadn't worked out that way. I hadn't allowed it to. Offering too much, I was scaring the hell out of her. What could she do but run away? And loving her as I did, what could I do but go after her?

That Friday I took my courage in my hands and drove to Amy's house. If Bob was there, and Amy told him to send me away . . . I was trembling as I drew up at the curb across from her house and checked her driveway. Thank God, luck seemed to be with me. Amy's white car was there, parked in the drive, but there was no sign of the old yellow van that Bob drove. This didn't mean much, however, as the van could easily be parked within the closed garage.

I climbed out of my car and slowly crossed the street. If only Amy would let me in, would talk to me.

Lesbian accosts former lover at her home, gets tossed

out by irate husband. *"She's thoughtless, possessive, sick, sick, sick!" says beautiful blond housewife. "Please, can't she be made to leave me alone?"*

But you love me, you love me! And I can't bear to give you up.

"So, out of the goodness of my heart, the kindness of my being, the sweetness of my soul, I made a dreadful mistake one weekend in the mountains, must I suffer for it forever?" wails childlike, doll-like blonde.

I was trembling as I stepped up onto the porch and rang the chime. I could hear it sounding inside. Would Amy answer the door, or would Bob?

Suddenly I wondered why I didn't turn around, leave, and allow the poor woman to live in peace. If I loved her as much as I claimed, why didn't I melt out of her life now as she so obviously wanted me to? To pursue her this way wasn't loving; it was thoughtless and selfish. I should leave this minute.

I lifted my hand and rang the bell a second time, knowing damn well that Amy was in there.

The door opened at last and Amy stood there, dressed in an old torn shirt and loose brown pants. "Oh, it's you," she wailed in dismay. One hand rose to press against her mouth. She blinked several times, obviously embarrassed and confused.

"May I come in?"

Amy hesitated, looking as though she wished she dared to tell me no, just go away, but after a moment she motioned me in. She kept her face turned away as she said, "I was just cleaning house. Would you like a cup of tea or something?"

My heart went out to her because she looked so embarrassed; I'd never seen her before when she wasn't perfectly made up. Each morning in the mountains I'd awakened before she had, and instinct had told me to leave the room and let her get up and get herself together before she had to face me. She'd mentioned once that she felt naked without eye makeup and that she rarely left the house without it, even if she was only going to the market. To be that concerned about appearance . . .

I felt swept through with sympathy for this woman I loved, who had allowed me to hold her and kiss her in the most intimate way but who could not face me now without mascara and eye shadow.

"No tea, thanks, but I would like a glass of water, please. I'm so scared my throat is dry."

"Scared?" Amy laughed, her eyes darting to me, then quickly away again. "Of me? Why? Did you think I'd throw you out or something?"

I shrugged, already feeling happy, sure that in coming here I'd done the right thing. "Well, I couldn't be sure. But I did want to talk to you."

Amy suggested we go out on the patio to have our drinks and talk. As we took our seats at the table there, she kept her face half turned away. Then within minutes she bounced up to say that she had to go to the store later and might as well get ready right then.

"Oh, for heaven's sakes, Amy," I said. "You don't have to make up for me. I love *you*, not your beautiful made-up face. Can't you relax with me even yet?"

Amy hesitated in the doorway into the house, then glanced back, throwing me her brilliant, childlike smile. "Sorry," she murmured, and hurried off.

In twenty minutes she was back, looking her usual self, the self I had always seen before. She'd changed her clothes, made up her face, and combed her hair. This time as she sat down she could face me fully, with her dimpled smile.

"So why did you come?" she asked brightly, like a friendly child.

"You know why. Because I love you. Because I haven't

seen you in so long. Because I want to know what's really bothering you so we can smooth it over and continue seeing each other."

"Oh, well," she said, "I suppose I knew you'd do this, but I thought you'd phone or write me. I didn't think you'd come to the house."

We sipped our drinks, our eyes caught, we smiled at each other, and I said, "So, what is the problem really? I can't believe you're breaking off just because I sent you a gift that cost a few dollars more than you thought it should."

Amy sighed. "No, I suppose not. It wasn't just that, it's everything. After all, I am married, and I feel so guilty—"

"Of course, I understand that."

Amy's eyes met mine. "But it's more than that. I just didn't realize what I was getting into, I guess. Letters, gifts, wanting to take me on trips. All you ever seem to think about is Amy, Amy, Amy, and Jane, I'm not worth it. There are millions of other people in the world, millions of other women, and you ought to go out to meet them and enjoy them."

"I love you," I said, and then I reached out, took her hand, and held it on the tabletop.

Amy sighed again. "Yes, I guess you do. I just didn't realize that everything would get so—messy and complicated. Wasting all that time and thought and money on me. I guess I just thought we could see each other for lunch once or twice a week, be warm and close and loving, maybe get together to make love every once in a while . . ." But she seemed to accept that this was not to be, that nothing in life is ever quite that simple, especially love.

I stayed for two hours, talking with her, and was still there when Bob got home after a visit to his doctor. He stuck his head through the patio doorway to say hello, looking and sounding very friendly, then he retreated into the house to leave us to talk some more.

Along about four that afternoon I got up to leave. Amy walked me to my car and kissed me good-bye, everything settled, nothing settled. We'd made a luncheon date for the following Tuesday.

From the next Tuesday on, we fell back into our pattern of lunching together two or three times a week, spending the entire afternoon together following lunch, talking, hugging, kissing, and as soon as school reopened and my house became available, Amy again drove over to climb excitedly into bed with me.

This was the woman whom I loved and I felt married to for life.

Seven

The Monday night after Amy's and my first daytime love-in in my home, I went barging into Russ's bedroom to make love with him, probably the first time in all our years together that I had deliberately initiated sex. When our elder son, Jason, had left for college four years before, Russ had moved into his bedroom. With advancing years, Russ was suffering more than ever from insomnia and was up and down five to ten times a night. I'd told him repeatedly that his movements in and out of bed didn't bother me, I could always fall back asleep, but it bothered him extremely to feel he was disturbing me, so the moment we had a spare bedroom he happily moved into it, and we'd been sleeping in separate bedrooms since.

During our years of marriage we had set up a sequence of signals, as I suppose every married couple does, indicating when we were interested in/agreeable to having sex. As Russ was far more interested in it than I, I left it up to him to make the overtures. If he wasn't interested, that was certainly all right with me. But during our years together I had rarely turned him down, once he had made his desires clear, had committed himself to wanting me. However, being a basically considerate person, Russ would almost always engage in playful preliminary jousting to give me a chance to retreat if I couldn't handle sex comfortably at the time. He had mentioned to me repeatedly that one of the things that had blown his first marriage was his strong and frequent need for sex, which he felt he had not kept adequately under control, and he didn't want this to happen with us; therefore, he would playfully indicate interest but without drawing his ego into it, without subjecting himself to hurt or rage if I wasn't in the mood.

Over the years we had dropped into this pattern, with few variations. If he had ideas, he would begin to express them from the moment he got home from work, patting me as I dished up dinner. Then, as dinner ended, he would mutter that he guessed he'd better go bathe and get dressed up to go out, as he felt in need of a woman.

If I gave him a hug and a kiss and said, "Go ahead, I'm so tired all I plan to do is bathe and dive into bed," Russ would bite my ear in revenge and that would be that.

Usually, though, I'd kid back that if it was all that much trouble to go out and find another woman, maybe he'd better settle for the one right here at home; and once our younger son, Tommy, was settled in bed for the night, I'd go to Russ's bedroom on cue. Since Russ could be counted on to issue his invitations with unfailing regularity, I saw no point in ever initiating things myself. I didn't feel he was in the least need of that kind of encouragement. But the night after Amy's first love-in visit to my home, I went barging into Russ's bedroom without invitation.

A part of my motivation was, unquestionably, guilt. Although Russ knew that I had strong lesbian interests, which he had encouraged for years, until Amy, I had never been unfaithful to him. If I had so much sexual interest that I would bed down with someone else, then surely he had a right to his share of my loving too.

But guilt alone wouldn't have been strong enough to propel me into his bedroom, breaking our long-established pattern. An equally strong motivation was that I was so sexually keyed up I needed release. Whenever I spent any time with Amy I became uncomfortably aroused. Going to bed with her pushed me over the brink; despite the two or three orgasms I'd experience during our lovemaking, I seemed unable to calm down afterward. So, though in my heart it rather appalled me, I went racing into my husband's arms only hours after I'd kissed Amy in warm, passionate good-bye.

Earlier in my life I would have sworn I couldn't cope with having two sexual love affairs concurrently; now I found that what I most wanted was to go from one to the other within a matter of hours, which is what I did the first half-dozen times Amy came to the house. One time I tried reversing it, making love with Russ the night before Amy was due over instead of following her visit, but that worked out far less successfully for me.

Fortunately, my feelings gradually subsided and I quit this pattern, which intellectually though not emotionally had definitely appalled me. From then on I did a better job of spacing my sexual encounters. By then Russ knew about Amy as Amy had always known about Russ, but neither ever asked me specifics about the other, for which I was deeply grateful. It certainly would have embarrassed me, back in the beginning, to admit to either one how brief a time had elapsed between my farewell kiss with the one and my hello kiss with the other.

Russ's first marriage had broken up, after years of bitter fights and recriminations over their differing ideas about life and time and money, when his wife began dating another man behind his back, which for Russ had been the final straw. He'd packed up and left, taking with him, as painfully heavy baggage, an apparently incurable fear of wifely infidelity. If a wife could do that to him after thirteen years of marriage, what certainty was there in anything? On numerous occasions Russ had looked me straight in the eye and proclaimed that he didn't have a jealous bone in his body, yet he'd blown up in fury any number of times in response to a careless comment on my part indicating some favorable response to another man.

Once, years before, when I'd first gotten into yoga, I'd stayed after class one night to enjoy a conversation about yoga with the teacher, who was a woman; another woman student had also participated, as well as a man student. When I told Russ about it, everything was fine and calm — until I got around to mentioning the last-named, a man, whereupon Russ had gone off like a time bomb.

"I knew it, I knew you were going to that class just to meet some man! If you're all that interested in him, go on down there and live with him! Go on, who needs you here —" On and on, while I listened in amazement, unable to believe that so little had set him off. But nothing, even total loyalty over the years, seemed to allay his underlying fear that someday I'd do the same thing his first wife had done.

One night he blew up about an unfortunate comment I'd made dealing with infidelity, and still furious the following morning, he had continued his harangue.

"I know you're just dying to have an affair, so go ahead; have one, who cares? If you have to have another man —" He ranted on, while I wondered, as I frequently did, where he found the energy, at his age, to become so angry so often over such trivial things.

"Oh, for heaven's sakes," I said finally, with complete calmness, "don't you know by now that I haven't the least interest in other men? If I'm ever unfaithful to you, it will be with another woman, not a man."

"Oh," Russ said, completely startled out of his anger. Nothing more was said for several moments; then, good humor entirely restored, he remarked, "Well, if I'm ever unfaithful to you, it will be with another woman also, not with a man."

Laughing, I walked over to him, and we kissed and made up.

Somehow, when we don't want to hear things or are afraid to believe what we hear, it takes forever before we give in. This wasn't the first time I had told Russ that my interest was in other women, not in men. But this seemed to be the first time he had ever actually taken it in. At least two years earlier, after reading a book about lesbians, I had remarked casually to him one evening that possibly I'd made a mistake, possibly I should have lived my life as a lesbian.

To my surprise, Russ responded instantly, firmly, "It's still not too late."

Startled, I laughed. "Oh, come on, of course it's too late."

Scowling, he walked over to me, took hold of my shoulders, and looked directly down into my eyes. "I never want to hear you say that again," he ordered. "It's never too late to do anything you really want to do."

Excited by his words, the thought striking me for the first time that he really might not mind if I became involved with another woman, I answered kiddingly, "What are you trying to say, that you don't want to stay married to me, that you wouldn't mind at all if I broke up our marriage and went off with a woman lover?"

A slight look of surprise and dismay ran through Russ's eyes, but he didn't back down. "I'm saying that I love you and want you to be happy." And he bent down to kiss me.

We had never really settled down and discussed it; there had simply been these random comments over the years, remarks leading me to believe that he wouldn't object to my indulging in a lesbian affair. I had never felt any need to pin him down more precisely, as it had all seemed so highly unlikely, and half the time I'd feel that I was out of my mind even to consider the possibility of any such thing.

By this point in our marriage Russ and I got along remarkably well, felt genuine affection and respect for each other, I enjoyed his company, our sex life together was fine, financially we were doing well, and, short of the nation's economy falling flat on its face, we could look forward, after decades of hard work, to reasonable financial security during our later years. Our five sons, Russ's three from his first marriage, and our two, were decent, responsible, bright, and apparently stable; we loved and were proud of them. What more could I possibly want from life?

Half the time I tended to answer that I didn't want anything more from life, I already had it all; I was healthy and happy and supremely content. But the rest of the time, deep inside there was a small ache, which grew larger and larger with time, and which told me I did want something more. I wanted to be physically and emotionally close to another woman. I wanted a woman to love and be loved by.

If Russ had been more of a socializer, possibly this ache would never have become so pronounced, but, fortunately or unfortunately, he never wanted to go anywhere or spend time with anyone. As he often reminded me, he spent his entire work life having to deal with people and by evening he was sick of it. All he wanted was to come home and relax in familiar surroundings, with no one around who didn't belong. And the only ones who belonged, in Russ's view, were Tommy and I now that all the older boys were gone.

When we were first married Russ and I occasionally went to a movie together, but this hadn't worked out because our tastes in movies were entirely dissimilar and one or the other of us would be painfully bored. We made no friends with whom to play cards or to have to dinner or to dine out with. In fact, we made no friends, period.

My socializing was primarily with my family, large family get-togethers that the boys and I attended, but Russ wouldn't go with us even on Christmas. And in all our years of marriage Russ and I have yet to attend a non-family party together, or even to take a weekend trip. The companionship we enjoy, and we do genuinely enjoy it, occurs entirely within the walls of our home.

In the early years my entertainment revolved primarily around our sons and their sports activities, in which Russ took absolutely no interest. Apart from that, I was chauffeur, babysitter, and general errand-parent for the sightseeing and short vacation trips the boys wanted to take, which of course we took without Russ. I always enjoyed these activities and trips, but with the passage of years the boys grew up, got their drivers' licenses, and developed social lives of their own, leaving me either to wither on the vine or go out to do likewise.

Whereas Russ has always worked away from home, dealing with people all day, I work at home, alone. Even when I work away from the house, cleaning, painting, and repairing our rental houses, I almost always work alone, which is fine. I prefer it that way. I like myself and almost never tire of being alone, yet occasionally I enjoy mingling with others, going places, socializing.

When I was left to my own devices after my sons outgrew me, my first solo venture away from the nest was to a weekly yoga class, which I thoroughly enjoyed and in which I made many friends. Women friends. In time I expanded further and joined the local NOW chapter, in which I made more women friends. In this way my life became fuller, happier. And Russ actively encouraged me, as though this lifted a burden from him. As long as I was having such a good time with my women friends, there was no need for him to go anywhere with me. Not that he ever had, but now he no longer had to feel an occasional twinge of guilt over it. And how could I get into any trouble, how could I put any strain on our marriage, as long as I was socializing only with other women?

As my social life, maybe lunch once or twice a week with my friends, plus an occasional evening out, began to expand and take shape, and as a bigger share of my enjoyment of life began to be derived from spending time with other women, my long-dormant lesbian feelings seemed to come back to life, to be reactivated. If it felt this good to be close to my friends, to laugh and talk with them, why not find that one special woman to be even closer to, to love and be loved by? Apparently Russ wouldn't mind. Though the thought frightened me, I knew it was something I wanted, would always want. So what was stopping me? Why not begin going to the Gay Center in town and start looking around?

So I did, and met no one I felt attracted to, until I joined a certain yoga class.

One Sunday morning several weeks after my weekend trip with Amy, by which time we were back to seeing each other regularly during the day, Russ brought up the subject of my trips down to the Gay Center, so I decided to ask him point-blank how he felt, to find out once and for all how much risk I was running with my marriage. I walked over to where he stood by the sink, looked up into his eyes, and said, "All right, Russ, let me put it to you straight out. If I were to have a sexual love affair with a woman, would you object?"

"No," he said, without hesitation or the blinking of an eye.

Though fully expecting this answer, and feeling anything but angry, I responded rather tartly, "And why wouldn't you mind?"

After a slight hesitation he said, "Because I love you and want you to be happy. I know that would make you happy, so I wouldn't mind."

Though I didn't question that this was the truth at that point in our relationship, I also knew that it was a generous and loving emotional position that Russ had been able to arrive at only after a good bit of conflict and pain.

A few years before, when I'd joined my first yoga class

and had made a fairly close woman friend, Susan, she and I, with her two children and my two sons, had gone to the mountains for a week's vacation. I'd taken the trip because Tommy had been complaining that we never went anywhere; all his friends went away on summer-vacation trips, but we never did. He wanted to go to the mountains, so I arranged the trip.

Russ of course flatly refused even to consider coming with us, not even for one weekend. At first I thought I'd be spending the week alone with Tommy, who was eleven; Jason, seventeen, ready to enter college in the fall, agreed to come but only for a day or two. He had too many social events scheduled to be willing to waste more time than that with his mother and little brother. Then, as I was making the arrangements, Susan mentioned that she'd love to come along with her two children, if I didn't mind. This suited me fine, and Russ seemed happy and relieved about it too, glad to know that I'd have adult companionship for the week.

The five of us, Jason staying only briefly, as planned, had a truly lovely and relaxing week, swimming, boating, hiking, and playing games. Susan remarked to me wistfully at least five times that it was absolutely marvelous to be away from her husband's angry tongue, if only for a few days. Their marriage broke up about eight months later. And I had to agree that it was wonderful being away from Russ's anger also; this was the very first time I'd been away longer than a weekend. The week passed idyllically, without an angry word except for a brief temper tantrum thrown by Susan's little boy, but neither of us minded much. It was the tantrums thrown by our fully grown husbands that were so terribly wearying. A quiet, soft, peaceful, utterly relaxing week, two grown women, three young children. But then the week drew to a close and we had to go home.

Upon Tommy's and my return, Russ greeted me with

the greatest affection. We settled down at the kitchen table to talk, over his glass of beer; he seemed entirely calm and accepting of the fact I'd been gone, and happy to hear that I'd had a wonderful week with Susan, without him. But shortly after our pleasant conversation had drawn to an end and I'd begun cleaning the kitchen, Russ found an excuse to blow up, following which he ranted and raved for what seemed like hours.

It was several years before I got another glimpse into the conflicts Russ was going through in his attempts to be as emotionally open and generous with me as he truly wanted to be. The year before I met Amy I had met a woman in a class, Vera, whom I've already mentioned; I felt immensely attracted to her, but when I dared to tell her how I felt, she dropped out of class.

About a month after this happened, I was in Russ's bedroom one night talking with him when he asked me why it was that I never mentioned Vera anymore. Immediately feeling sad all over again about what had happened, on impulse I gave Russ a brief rundown on it, telling him about my feelings for Vera, my confession of those feelings, and her shocked repudiation. Russ listened quietly, his eyes expressing great emotional support. Then when I ended he put his arm around me and murmured, "Poor baby," seeming not in the least upset.

But, in spite of his apparent acceptance, he hadn't taken it all that calmly. Hours after I'd fallen asleep, I heard him prowling around the house, making far more noise than he usually did, as though not averse to waking me. So I sleepily crawled out of bed and wandered out to ask him what the problem was.

"Well, goddammit," he snapped, "I've looked absolutely everywhere but I can't find my seed catalog anywhere. Do you happen to know where the hell it is?"

Two o'clock in the morning and he was prowling the

house for a seed catalog, which turned out to be right on the shelf where we always kept it, but Russ hadn't been able to find it there.

If I was interested in other women, if I became sexually involved with another woman, wouldn't this shut him out? Symbolically, wouldn't his seed get lost? He needed reassurance from me.

Apparently the anxiety this caused him gradually grew less deep-seated, because one night in his bedroom he openly expressed his fear. We'd been discussing a recent trip of mine to the Gay Center, and I'd been telling him about various women I'd met there, when suddenly Russ looked anxiously at me and commented, "You know, Jane, if you do find someone, some woman you like, some woman to be lovers with, well, what do I do then?"

Before I could answer, he put his arm around me, drew me close, and said with affectionate firmness, "Well, never mind, somehow we'll work it out," a comment that moved me deeply. He seemed determined to give me ample leeway to find the experience I so hungrily sought, while he clung to the belief that whatever problems arose, we'd work them out somehow.

I occasionally wondered if aside from Russ's very real love for me, there was another, unconscious factor motivating him. A few years earlier I'd become very close, warm friends with a woman named Helen, whose husband, Stuart, was twenty years older than she and all but completely impotent. Eventually I had come to the realization that Stuart was trying to push me into physical intimacies with his wife, which made me feel deeply sympathetic toward him in what I considered his fear-ridden plight. He knew that he wasn't sexually satisfying his wife, as did everyone else who knew Helen. She talked about it openly to almost everyone, making frequent, biting jokes. Stuart loved Helen and couldn't bear the thought of losing her, and apparently he saw me as a far safer lover for her than another man would be. If she took up with another man, what was to stop her from leaving Stu and plunging into an exciting new marriage? But if she took up with me instead, well, after all, I had a husband and children to consider, just as Helen did. So why couldn't the two of us just quietly have a sexual love affair without ripping apart anyone's marriage?

Helen and I were both too inhibited to take advantage of Stuart's nudges, and before I'd become free and unrepressed enough, to the point where I might really have given it a try, Stuart had died of a stroke and Helen and her children had left the West Coast, to return to her parents' home.

Russ, though not in any way impotent yet, was nevertheless ten years older than I, and also, I knew from numerous conversations, absolutely convinced of the rapacious sexuality of the female. Left sexually unsatisfied, women always went on the prowl; this was a cardinal article of faith with Russ. I often wondered if this wasn't the source of much of his sexual drive, the unconscious fear that if he wasn't always on the sexual ready he wouldn't be able to keep a woman, first his first wife, then me, satisfied. If he felt that if he became impotent as he got older, I was bound to wander away from him, to seek satisfaction elsewhere; surely it would be less threatening to his ego if I did this straying with other women. Russ likes and appreciates women, sees them as strong and intelligent, generally far more trustworthy than men, and far more beautiful. As long as I confined my wandering to other women, possibly he could relax a bit and begin to feel a slight bit less pressured sexually. So once Russ had dealt with and pretty well conquered his underlying fears, he could answer me with a good bit of honesty that it was all right with him if I found a woman lover.

After he'd said that he wouldn't mind, I commented, "Of course you don't mind. It's just what the women at the gay rap sessions say—men don't object to lesbian affairs because they don't see them as being serious. If there's no penis involved it's only play, it's not serious or important sex. The only serious sex is sex with a penis."

"That's not true!" Russ protested, his cheeks flushing. "I do look upon it as serious, but I still wouldn't mind."

I made no further comment on whether sex minus a penis can be serious. In my view, as drawn toward the homosexual world as I have always been, it isn't. Surely the only thing that makes sex "serious" is the possibility of pregnancy, or, secondarily, bodily injury. The tongue, the lips, and the fingers are harmless indeed compared to an erect penis. Without threat of either pregnancy or bodily hurt, how could sex, as normally practiced between two women, ever be anything serious?

One of the many really lovely things I've learned from Amy is that when approached happily, freely, and in a childlike spirit of play, it sure can be a whole lot of fun.

The fact that the sex itself is playful and nonthreatening certainly doesn't mean that the love affair can't be serious—deeply, wonderfully serious. Possibly, even, love can flow more easily, more richly, simply because the sex is so nonthreatening.

Going to bed with Amy was play, but loving her was very serious, as deep and meaningful an emotion as I had ever experienced.

Later that same day, as Russ and I were having lunch, he suddenly remarked, his face flushing, "You've told me about Pat and Leslie, how they feel about this lesbian thing, and about Lois and Sherry"—a lesbian couple I knew— "and about Joy," she was my recently divorced heterosexual friend, "but you haven't ever said a word about Amy. How does she feel about it?"

Jumping up and hurrying to the sink, I busily began rinsing off my plate. I replied airily, "Oh, hell, Russ, I don't know. I don't discuss it with every friend I have, you know, so I haven't the least idea how she feels."

"Oh," he said, sounding disappointed. Then the subject was dropped.

I had to face how terribly curious Russ must have been about my newly developed "friendship" with Amy, otherwise he wouldn't have asked about her. While he always listens attentively to anything I tell him, he rarely asks questions. This has been true all the years I've known him. Even when he goes to a doctor, he won't ask the essential questions; he'd rather know little or nothing about what the doctor discovered than risk asking a question. Yet now he'd opened up enough to ask about Amy.

After I'd answered with such an out and out lie, I felt ashamed of myself. I had never asked Amy how she would feel if I told Russ about us, but I doubted that she would mind; it seemed only fair, as she certainly knew about him.

After thinking about it all afternoon, I went into Russ's bedroom that evening. He was sitting on the edge of his bed, undressing to take a bath. I pressed my hand on his leg, aware that I was blushing slightly, and said, "Honey, when you asked about Amy earlier today, well, I don't know why I lied but I did. I *have* discussed my lesbian feelings with her, and she has them too. The fact is . . . ," a momentary hesitation before I could get it out, "I'm in love with her and we're having an affair."

"Oh," Russ said. He put his arm around me, pressed me close, and said, "If it's making you happy, honey, then I'm glad."

We sat for quite a time that way, pressed together, with Russ's arm about me, not saying anything more, just being close and companionable. It might not work out, but at least we seemed off to a reasonably hopeful start.

Eight

In the months that followed, Amy and I seemed to fall ever more deeply in love. Before meeting her, I had worried that if I did fall in love with some woman I might get so carried away I would leave Russ, or else feel miserably trapped and unhappy because I couldn't. Instead, I found I handled my double life, my multiple loves, with no great problem; the more deeply I loved Amy, the happier I felt and the more enjoyment I felt in loving Russ and Tommy too. And throughout this period Amy seemed to be handling her double life equally well.

Our summer yoga class had come to an end even before our weekend trip. In late September, when the new school year began, we enrolled in a class at a local junior college; it met two nights a week, from eight to ten. Amy's house was right on the way for me, so I always picked her up for class. After class we'd stop for something to eat, arriving back at her house sometime after eleven. Then we'd sit in the car, in the dark, talking, holding hands, embracing, kissing, until midnight or after, until finally, with one final good-night kiss, Amy would climb out and I'd watch her walk to the side door of her home and disappear inside.

During these months Amy slowly began to drop her defenses and tell me about her childhood, a miserable time during which her parents had made her feel both unloved and unwanted while showering attention and affection on her younger brother. No matter how desperately she had tried to be good, to keep a beaming smile on her face and never act angry or jealous, she had never been able to win her parents' love. She told me of one incident, which had occurred after she had married and become the mother of two children, in which her mother had hurt her feelings so badly that in telling me about it, twenty years after the hurt had been inflicted, Amy broke down and cried. Made to feel unlovable in childhood, she had never really gotten over the feeling that she didn't deserve to be loved.

During these months Amy also began to get more in touch with some of her negative feelings toward Bob. More than once she angrily denounced him to me, spitting out scorn and resentment.

One day when we had a luncheon date, her car was being repaired so I drove to her home to pick her up. When she met me at the door and asked me in, I saw at once that she wasn't ready; she hadn't even started. Dressed in sloppy old clothes, hair uncombed, eyes red from weeping, she looked a mess. Murmuring that she was sorry but couldn't possibly go to lunch with me, she crumpled down on the end of the sofa and began to cry.

"What's the matter?" I asked, sitting beside her and taking her hand.

"What isn't the matter?" Amy countered, her eyes, swollen and streaked, flashing up to meet mine. "I'm in such a mess—how did I ever get into this?" Weeping harder, she again hid her face.

She never did explain what mess she was in, though

from the few hints she dropped I gathered that by "mess" she meant simply her life in general, her relationship with Bob, their financial situation. She hadn't eaten in twenty-four hours, she told me; she was far too angry and upset to feel like eating.

"Angry at Bob?" I asked, and after only a very slight hesitation she emphatically nodded her head. Yes, of course, angry at him.

Yet, within a very few minutes, when we heard the teakettle in the kitchen begin to whistle, Amy dutifully got up to fix Bob a cup of tea, and once she'd fixed it she carried it out to the patio and very lovingly called out to him that his tea was ready and she would set it on the patio table for him, acting and sounding for all the world like the happiest, most devoted wife.

When she came back in, she offered me a cup of tea too, but I told her I was hungry and ready for lunch. A sudden look in Amy's eyes tipped me off that she felt hungry enough, and was throwing off her anger enough, to be ready for lunch too.

"Sure you don't want to come with me?" I asked.

Two seconds of wavering, then, "If you'll give me ten minutes to get ready . . ."

Apart from Russ, who can go from friendly kidding into violent anger and back again in one second flat, I'd never known anyone who could switch moods as fast as Amy, from a deeply troubled, despairing woman to a bright happy child, and back again. And this was unquestionably one of the things about her that most enchanted me.

One day sometime later Amy arrived at my house so angry at Bob that she couldn't wait to blow up about him. That morning she had juiced some green vegetables, taken from Russ's garden with great appreciation, and had poured out a tiny little quarter of a glass, trying to get Bob to drink it.

"I put carrots in it too, you know, to sweeten it," Amy

told me, "and it was *so* good, so delicious, you could just feel the lifegiving force in it, but do you think he'd drink it, even a mouthful? Well, that's it, I'll never try again. He can drop dead tomorrow, for all I care."

She was nude in my bed by this time, resting against the headboard, reaching out her arms to me even as she said this.

Laughing, I said, "Oh yes you would, sweetheart. You *would* care."

"No, no, I wouldn't," Amy insisted, drawing me close. "He can drop dead this minute and I wouldn't even care." Then we began to make love.

No more did Amy refer to Bob in a soft, loving voice as that "dear, sweet man," as she had repeatedly when we first met. Now whenever she mentioned him it was almost always to express irritation, largely in regard to what she saw as his stupid unwillingness to take proper care of himself.

"He wants to be sick, he enjoys it. He likes to rush off to see his doctor every other day; so what if he's running up big doctor bills, he should care, he's not the one who has to worry about getting them paid," Amy would sometimes rant, though she'd soon run down, sigh, and get over the worst of her anger.

I saw Bob infrequently during this period, but he was always extremely courteous and friendly, always seemed to be the "dear, sweet man" Amy had at first said he was, but I didn't doubt that he, like the rest of us, was a complex person, and, in numerous ways that only the woman who lived with him would know, a royal pain.

But Amy was not comfortable with ambivalence. As she grew more secure in our relationship, she could begin to face and express anger at Bob; but now that she and I were in love, she didn't dare get angry or upset with me. I was the new "dear, sweet" person in her life, to whom she was utterly devoted.

While she couldn't handle ambivalent feelings as well

as I could, Amy could far more easily and unself-consciously express affection physically, whether in the simple act of holding my hand in public, greeting me with a friendly kiss in front of her husband, or in the most intimate sexual caresses. These things she did as freely, innocently, and spontaneously as a child, in a way that at first I found a trifle embarrassing, then began to envy, and in time tried hard to emulate. Whereas during our first weekend in the mountains when Amy had reached for my hand to hold as we walked and I'd soon found some excuse to draw it free again, by the time we'd been lovers for a few months I was able, with almost no self-consciousness, to hold hands with her when walking down the main street in the small town in which we live. A small success, no doubt, but to me an important one.

In late September I was called to jury duty, and while I was serving, Amy frequently drove down to share my long lunch period with me. We'd usually meet in front of the restaurant in which we ate, and as I'd see her walking toward me, head high, blond hair flying, with that lovely, jaunty walk of hers, my heart would all but burst with love. We'd meet, both of us grinning, and embrace and kiss. And surely life has no more joy to offer than I knew in those moments.

In yoga class one night the teacher quizzed the students as to who was taking the course for credit, and Amy learned that I had graduated from college, which greatly impressed her. She began voicing astonishment that the two of us had gotten together, asked me what I was doing hanging around with a "dumbie" like her, insisted—once again—that she wasn't good enough for me, and that on top of being dumb she was also "worthless, rotten, and no good." Though I often tried laughingly to get her to tell me in what way she was these things, she always just smiled rather sadly and shrugged, and assured me that in time I'd find out what a mean, worthless bitch she was.

Early in October, after being released from jury duty for the day, I drove to a savings and loan office a few blocks from Amy's home and made arrangements to open an account; I wanted to deposit in it the six hundred dollars I had saved, as I'd told Amy I was going to, toward the cost of her carpeting. To open a joint account I needed her signature on a small card I was given, and I also needed her mother's maiden name.

That night, before the start of yoga class, as we sat on the grass outside the building, I asked Amy to sign the card. She dutifully signed, but as she did so she asked me what the card was for. Not wanting to tell her about it before the account was safely open, I lied, offering a vague explanation about needing to use her as a reference, and she seemed to accept this. I figured that after class, when we stopped to have something to eat, I'd start up a conversation about our respective mothers and get her to tell me her mother's maiden name.

Amy outsmarted me, however, for as we walked toward the small restaurant we usually went to after class, she suddenly told me that she didn't believe my story about the card she had signed for me. She knew what I was up to, she said, smiling gaily at me. I was being sneaky in much the same way as she often was with Bob, primarily in secretly mixing healthy ingredients into the junk food he ate. But I couldn't fool her that easily, she assured me.

I laughed uneasily, taking her at her word, sure that she had figured it out, so, once we got seated in the restaurant and had put in our order, I drew out the card and asked her straight out what her mother's maiden name was.

"Szzmik," Amy responded immediately, spelling it for me, then her eyes narrowed suspiciously. "But why do you ask? I never heard of needing that just for a reference. The only time anybody asks that is when you're opening a bank account."

Blushing, I said, "But I thought you said you'd figured it out! I thought you knew that's what I'm doing, but it's not a bank account, it's a savings account. I told you I planned to save six hundred dollars by October first, which I have, and I'm opening this account to deposit the money in. I want you to keep the passbook so that if you ever need any money you'll be able to take it out. And if you don't need it, then we'll use it toward the carpeting in December."

Amy's chin began to quiver, then her lips. "But, Jane, I told you if I needed money I'd let you know." Her eyes were beginning to glisten with tears. "So why are you doing this?"

"So you won't have to ask me. I don't want you to have to ask me. I want it to be there if you need it, if any emergency arises or whatever."

Amy began to cry, lowering her face and pressing one hand over her mouth. After a few moments she lifted her eyes again, wet with tears, and said, as though in genuine agony, "But, Jane, I *love you* , don't you understand?" Her mouth and chin were quivering so much that she could barely talk.

"But that isn't in question," I said, beginning to feel sick and miserable myself because Amy seemed so upset. "I know you love me, and I love you, and because I love you I don't want you to feel dependent on me, don't want you to have to come to me and ask me for money if you need it. I just want you to take the passbook and keep it and help yourself anytime you need whatever's in there."

"No!" Amy said, crying even harder.

She was so upset that before long I said that if the whole idea disturbed her so much, then I wouldn't do it. I hadn't been trying to cause her pain, that was the last thing I'd had in mind; I'd only been trying to help.

Eventually Amy calmed down, stopped crying, and we began to sip the juice drinks the waitress had brought us; one of Amy's hands was holding one of mine tightly on the tabletop. I'd felt so happy and pleased opening the account that afternoon, and now I felt blue. Was what I'd tried to do really such a lousy thing to do to my love?

As I drove us home later I reached over to hold Amy's hand. She immediately clasped my hand tightly in both of hers, then lifted it to her mouth to kiss my palm, something she hadn't ever done before. "You're so sweet," she murmured, kissing my hand a second time.

In the driveway of her home we sat and talked for quite some time, embracing and kissing; at last she climbed out and started into the house, then swung around suddenly and walked back to the car. I hastily rolled down my window, and she stuck her head inside and murmured again, "Jane, you're so sweet," and kissed me good-night one final, final time.

As I drove home I felt happy again, full of my love, and after I'd bathed and climbed into bed I still felt full of her, she'd never seemed so close. After I drifted off to sleep I dreamed of her, a lovely warm dream. And when I woke in the morning I had flipflopped again, deciding that I would go ahead with opening the account after all; in spite of Amy's tearful protests, brought on by her fears and insecurities, I felt that she had been deeply pleased by what I'd told her I was doing.

That afternoon, after jury duty, I drove to the savings and loan office, handed in the little card, and opened the joint account for us. At first Amy didn't want to take possession of the passbook, but in time she gave in and tucked it into her purse, where it stayed, untouched, Amy being Amy, for the next few weeks. But nevertheless it gave me a nice feeling to know that she had it, that if things got financially rough enough for her she might even break down and withdraw a dollar or two.

On election day I was scheduled to work all day at the headquarters of a woman running for the state assembly, and, at my urging, Amy came down to have lunch with me. As we were walking around after eating, watching the time, I handed her a colorful brochure, which I'd picked up at a travel agency, describing various Caribbean cruises. As she first took the brochure from me she flashed me a mildly reproachful, flirtatious look, which I ignored, telling her that I still wanted to take the trip the following year, hopefully in the late spring, after April taxes were safely paid. I felt that in order to take the cruise then we might have to make reservations as early as December; therefore, I wished she'd look the brochure over and decide whether she would come with me.

"Well, if you insist," Amy murmured, eyes full of love even as she tried to look dismayed at my stubbornness. "I'll look it over tonight."

Soon after that I had to return to my election-day telephone duties, and Amy walked me to the entryway and offered me a warm good-bye kiss before turning to leave.

When I phoned her the next day, she announced excitedly that she had not only looked at the brochure, she had read it from cover to cover, and — "I'm ready to pack right now, when do we leave?"

"Hey, great," I said, joy spurting through me, but worry too. Would I be able to afford all these goodies I was so eager to offer my love? "I have to spend all day tomorrow over at the office, but let's talk it over Friday at lunch, all right?"

"Fine," Amy said, and our conversation veered to other things.

When she arrived at my house on Friday, after she'd stepped inside and kissed me she handed me back a brochure on Caribbean cruises, but not the one I'd given her.

"I meant to bring yours back today," she explained quickly, "but I forgot, so I stopped at a travel agent's and picked up this one, which is next year's, showing the new rates. And, Jane, you wouldn't believe it, the rates for next year jump out of sight. Look, look here."

Flipping the book open, she showed me a page on which she had jotted down figures and added them up. I didn't realize that Amy had picked and added the wrong figures. As I glanced at the figures I was appalled. The way Amy had figured it, the price of the cruise was going to increase more than three hundred dollars per person, so even the cheapest rooms were over nine hundred dollars per person for the seven-day cruise.

Immediately more than a little scared by this, I glanced again at the figures, but only momentarily, then tossed the brochure down and suggested that we go have lunch and afterward look over the figures and decide what to do.

In the restaurant, Amy suggested that maybe we shouldn't go at all, unless there was some way we could go before the end of the year, before the rate increase. "But I don't suppose you'd have the money in time?" she questioned rather hesitantly.

"Well, even if I could get the money," I said (but from where? and what would Russ think?), "I doubt very much if we could get reservations this late."

"Oh, you think so?" Amy said, not able to hide her disappointment.

"Well," I suggested, "as soon as we've finished eating, let's walk down to the travel agent's and see whether or not we can."

As we walked down to the travel agency Amy was happier and more excited than I'd ever seen her before. "Oh, I'm sure we'll be able to get tickets," she assured me, tightly squeezing my hand.

"You really do want to go, don't you?" I countered, surprised and pleased at how excited she was.

"Oh, I've always loved to travel," she told me. "I'm ready to rush home and pack this minute. I'm already trying to figure out what clothes to take! And what costume to fix for the masquerade. I've got this Hawaiian skirt I brought back from Hawaii, and —"

As Amy talked on, laughing, grinning, beaming, looking and sounding like a ten-year-old, I began to hope fervently that we'd be able to get reservations for before Christmas, not for myself so much but because she was so excited. I'd had the brochure in my possession for several weeks before I'd finally dared to give it to Amy, not even glancing at it all the time I'd had it, while Amy, as soon as I'd put it into her hands, had read every word. The difference, I guess, between an incurable traveler and a basically happy stay-at-home.

As excited as Amy was, I nevertheless did my best to pin her down as to whether she was sure she would rather go on the cruise than get her new carpeting by Christmas; she was unwaveringly sure. "So who really cares about carpeting?" she insisted. "Taking this trip will give us wonderful memories we'll have for the rest of our lives!"

It was several months before I finally knew Amy well enough to realize that she probably would have preferred the carpeting, but that was something she saw as entirely for herself, and therefore, at that point in our relationship, verboten. The cruise was something we'd both enjoy; I would be getting some return on the money I spent.

Before long we were sitting in front of the travel agent's desk. He asked which starting date we were interested in.

Amy and I agreed that we didn't want to be gone during Christmas week, so we decided the best time would be the week before. While the agent put in a call to ask about reservations, we waited, waited, Amy glancing anxiously around at me, flashing me worried smiles. Then finally the man said thank you and hung up the phone.

"Well, they can't say at this time which room you'll be in, but they can guarantee to have a room for you when the time comes. Are you interested in that?"

Excited, worried, pleased, scared, I glanced around at Amy, to find her eyes hanging hopefully and anxiously on me, over the top of her glasses, which she'd put on to glance through another brochure. Taking my nerve in my hands, I said, "Yes, we're interested," and drew out my checkbook.

I asked the agent if he could possibly hold the check until the following Monday; this was a Friday. "If you bank it today, it won't clear," I told him somewhat anxiously. "I have to transfer money from a savings account before the check will be good."

"Understood," the man said, nodding. But would Russ understand?

After we left the agency Amy talked even more excitedly, repeatedly reaching over to hug me as we walked, while I, though recovering somewhat from the initial shock of what I'd done, continued to feel deeply uneasy. Never before had I acted so impulsively, writing out a check for that amount of money without even consulting Russ. And, on top of that, I simply wasn't used to such expensive self-indulgence. I'd never in my life taken a real vacation solely because I wanted to. To take this trip now, flying off with my love . . .

"What's the matter, Jane?" Amy asked later, after we'd reached the park and were resting there, talking. "You don't seem very happy about this. Don't you want to go?" I could see the first uneasiness beginning to creep into her eyes.

I looked at her lying there on her back on the grass, her lovely face flushed with excitement, her blue eyes rather worriedly searching mine, and in that moment all regret rolled out of me and I was wonderfully pleased at what we were doing.

"Of course I want to go," I said softly. "I feel just a slight bit stunned by the suddenness of it, but aside from that I'm truly pleased. I love you, Amy." Then I leaned over to kiss her, giving her barely enough time to say, "I love you too," before my mouth pressed down on hers.

Nine

It was the first regularly scheduled commercial flight I had ever taken. My only previous experience flying had been a few years earlier when my two sons and I had gone up for a fifteen-minute aerial view of San Gabriel Valley in a small plane out of El Monte airport.

When we'd told Russ about it at dinner that night, his face had gone white. "My God, why didn't you tell me beforehand?" he'd exclaimed. "I'd have been worried sick."

Russ is an expert worrier, having had years and years of experience. When he can't find anything in our personal life to worry about, or in his business, he reaches out and worries about other people's problems, sometimes people we scarcely know.

Once when my sister and her husband were planning something that upset him, he voiced endless worry about it, lost sleep, stalked the house in the wee hours of the morning, and repeatedly "ordered" me to get on the phone and tell her not to do it; finally I lost all patience with him.

No matter how *he* felt about it, I blew up at him, it was their business, their problem, their decision, and I certainly had no intention of trying to interfere or of worrying about it.

That was just like me, Russ shot back; I simply refused to carry my share of the worry load, forcing him to worry for both of us.

Though I am not by nature a worrier and rarely lose sleep over anything, I had more than my share of anxious moments before Amy and I finally left on our trip.

First, of course, I worried about having to tell Russ about what I'd done. I figured that Amy and I could withdraw the money from our newly opened account to cover our pocket money, but I still had to cover the check I'd written, and I wasn't willing to tap our savings account without Russ's knowledge.

So, the night after we'd made the reservations, I went into Russ's bedroom, faced him, and told him. He was wonderful about it. He acted genuinely pleased and excited for me, repeatedly commenting that he was sure Amy and I would have a fantastic time.

"Honey, I'm glad, I'm really glad," he must have told me at least five times, and from that moment until the time we said good-bye at the airport, he never once wavered. Rather, he seemed almost as excited about the trip as Amy was.

One worry down, only a few hundred left to deal with.

The few times I mentioned to Russ how worried I felt, he immediately reassured me that flying was easy, nothing to feel the least concerned about. If I'd just unbend a bit and have a couple of drinks before boarding the plane, then a drink or two on board, I'd sail through the experience benumbed and unworried.

Russ's reassurances didn't really help, as they didn't in any way address my real concerns, which I was keeping to myself. I didn't have a single moment's uneasiness about the flight. What worried me was the trip itself.

Up to that point Amy and I had seen each other only

under the most stress-free circumstances. Apart from our all-too-brief weekend trip to the mountains, we saw each other only a few hours at a time, during which we were surely on our best, most loving behavior. We lunched together, attended yoga class together, and on lovely special occasions Amy would drive over and we'd hurry into my already darkened bedroom to dive into bed and make love. Under such a romantic regime it was little wonder that we'd never really gotten angry at each other, never gotten into anything resembling a no-holds-barred argument. But, eight days together?

Two things worried me most. One, that in short order, thrown together to share a small cabin on the boat, we might easily become irritated and thoroughly disillusioned with each other. Before the eight days were up, would we even be speaking to each other? During the months I'd known her Amy had repeatedly voiced the sentiment, a commonly accepted opinion, that two people never really know each other until they begin living together. And once two people do begin living together, according to Amy, love is bound to be the first casualty, it immediately flies out the window.

I'd heard this expressed often in my life and tended to agree with it; certainly romantic love when put to the test often fails to survive. Just a few years earlier I'd read the cynical comment that there is one sure cure for falling in love: marriage. When I read this to Russ, he replied angrily that that was nonsense. He was more in love with me now than the day we'd married.

I knew very few people I could imagine happily spending even twenty-four hours with, much less eight days. But then, there was only one person I was madly in love with, and that was Amy. Would I still feel the same when we returned? Would she?

The other thing I worried about was that, as crazy as I already was about her, I might fall even more in love with her during our trip and wouldn't be able to bear going home. I remembered the depression that had hit me as I entered my home following our weekend together. If that was doubled, or trebled, would I be able to handle it? Or would my heart rebel and insist upon doing something crazy, like leaving home and running away with my love?

I'd been raised by a mother who loved to quote the line, *Stern Daughter of the Voice of God! O Duty!* and I loved the line myself. Since earliest childhood it had been instilled in me that while doing our duty might not make us happy, it was the only chance for happiness we had. And, in spite of the fact that such a belief is not currently in fashion, I had not yet seen any reason to abandon it. Just as Amy so often commented when we kidded about running off together, there was no way we could build our own happiness on the unhappiness of others. It wouldn't be fair to up and leave our husbands, who were raising no objections to our spending time and love on each other. Above all, I felt that leaving Russ, breaking up our home, wouldn't be fair to Tommy. In giving birth to him I had committed myself to doing the best I could for him. So, as long as Russ and I lived together with mutual respect and affection, and without too many unpleasant upheavals, I could not throw everything over in order to more conveniently indulge my romantic passion for Amy.

In my heart I didn't believe that the moment would actually arrive when the two of us would board a plane, fly off to Florida, and then set sail into the blue for a week's endless time together. All those minutes, hours, days together, it seemed too much to hope for.

Surely some emergency would arise to stop us. Bob would get sick: that's the primary stop-the-cruise emergency I foresaw. Or Amy would get sick, or Russ, or Tommy. In any case, *something* would stop us.

I once asked Tommy whether he would come on the trip with me if Amy couldn't. He said no way. I told Russ that if the worst came to pass and Amy couldn't go, he'd have to come with me. No way, he said. I frequently thought of phoning the travel agent to ask about a refund or postponement if it turned out we couldn't go.

But nothing happened to stop us, and on the scheduled night we were at the airport, Amy and I, with Russ, Tommy, and several other members of my family there to see us off. After we got our seat reservations and it was announced that the plane was ready for boarding, I stood leaning back against Russ, telling him I was too scared to go and that he was going to have to push me onto the plane.

"Nonsense," Russ said, taking hold of me by both arms and gently pushing me forward. "There's nothing to be scared of, honey. Just have a drink as soon as you can on board and you'll do just fine."

I straightened up, glanced around to smile at him one last time, threw Tommy a good-bye kiss, and followed Amy through the doorway and down the ramp to the plane.

Once we were settled down into our back-row seats, all my anxieties vanished. Glancing around at Amy, I felt incredibly happy and excited, ready to have the time of my life. Amy, noticing, grinned at me, then leaned over to kiss me. Eight days of steady togetherness coming up.

The flight was smooth, the landing easy. After being taken to a nearby hotel, we rested for a time in our room, then got ready to join the other passengers for lunch.

After a delicious buffet lunch at a lovely restaurant overlooking Biscayne Bay, Amy and I went for a walk, then settled down on a stone wall to talk. I told her that I thought there was something we should discuss before boarding the ship. Sharing a cabin for a week, we were going to be thrown into greater closeness than we'd yet experienced and it might easily happen that we'd become irritated with each other over minor habits we had. If this happened, I thought it important that we air such irritations as they arose.

"Amy, listen," I said, quite urgently. "I've known

people all my life who have a terrible time feeling or expressing anger, who hold it in till maybe weeks or months later, and then suddenly they explode and start yelling about what happened months before. And I have a very strong feeling that you're like that. That if you get to feeling angry at me over something I do, you won't tell me, you'll just hold it in, allowing it to fester until it poisons everything. So let's make an agreement right now that if either of us gets angry with the other, we'll express it and clear the air as soon as it happens, all right?"

Amy sat looking steadily at me, smiling indulgently as though I were the town idiot. "All right, but I know it's not going to happen. I love you, Jane."

"And I love you. But just because we love each other doesn't mean we can't get angry at each other," I insisted.

"Of course not," Amy agreed, then leaned over to kiss me, with a melting look in her eyes that said there was no way in this world she could ever be angry at me.

Shortly thereafter we decided to catch the tram over to the ship and go aboard.

As we walked toward the ship I felt exultant; a promise I'd made to myself was coming true. When I'd first met Amy I'd happened to mention that some friends of mine were just returning from a Caribbean cruise, and she had remarked rather wistfully that she'd always wanted to take such a cruise. Like any other half-crazed, wildly in love would-be lover, I'd snatched up this tidbit and made an immediate mental note of it, vowing to myself that someday I'd give my love her heart's desire. I'd take her on that cruise.

Even after I got to know Amy better and learned that she'd traveled quite extensively, far more than I had—she'd been to Europe, Mexico, South America, and to Hawaii four times, while I'd rarely spent even a day away from home—I didn't ask myself why she hadn't previously taken a cruise if that's what she'd always wanted to do. I had just felt that this was a heaven-sent opportunity for me to express my devotion to her.

As we walked toward the ship Amy suddenly told me the reason she had never taken a cruise before was that she always got violently seasick.

"My God," I said, stopping in my tracks and erupting into appalled laughter, "now you tell me!"

"But don't worry about it," she assured me. "It's just a question of mind over matter, right? And I don't plan to ruin our trip by allowing myself to get seasick this time."

"Though you always have before," I said. "On any kind of boat?"

Amy nodded. "Which is why I've never taken a cruise before. But don't worry about it," she repeated, walking forward again. "I'll be fine."

"God, I hope so."

Laughing, shaking my head in disbelief, I tagged along behind her as we boarded the ship.

We had left Los Angeles just before midnight on a Friday night, arrived in Miami Saturday morning, boarded the cruise ship fairly early Saturday afternoon, and set out to sea at four o'clock that afternoon.

Until Sunday evening Amy did fine. Then we ran into rough seas, the boat began rolling badly, everywhere you looked there were people clamping hands over their mouths and rushing to grab barf bags, which were displayed prominently on every railing. After dinner that evening Amy and I were in the lounge, watching a show, when she excused herself to go to the restroom. She was gone so long that I began to get worried, but before the anxiety had mounted to where I was ready to go off in search of her, she came back, looking a bit pale. But when I asked her if she was all right she assured me that she was. It wasn't until about two hours later, when we were back in our cabin, that she admitted that she had left the lounge show to go heave up her dinner.

"But I'm fine now," she said confidently. "I know I'll do fine."

By morning she felt reasonably well and did not throw up again. Mind over matter . . . or, love will prevail?

Until Tuesday afternoon, about halfway through the trip, we had a truly wonderful time. We'd bought tickets for tours in each of the ports of call, and we thoroughly enjoyed them.

We'd heard from friends who'd taken the trip that the meals aboard ship were fabulous, and they certainly were lavish, but unfortunately they were not to Amy's liking. By the second meal I was glad that, though we had a table for four, we had no tablemates. Amy, reading the menu, would begin to mutter and would go on to complain throughout the meal. Nothing suited her. By our second day at sea, both our waiter and our steward knew that they had a couple of oddballs at table 6. I ordered vegetables only, without complaint, while Amy, in a querulous voice, repeatedly asked if she couldn't have substitutes for what was offered. But the two of them, like the truly fine gentlemen they were, doing their best to keep us happy, in short order were automatically bringing Amy fresh fruit for every meal, never mind what was on the menu. A thoughtfulness for which Amy thanked them with beaming smiles.

Monday morning we went on a raft ride down the Rio Grande River in Port Antonio, Jamaica; Tuesday morning we climbed Dunn's River Falls in Ocho Rios, Jamaica. Amy had seemed to enjoy both excursions, as I most certainly had, but then as we were being led on a guided tour through the Shaw Park Gardens before returning to the boat in Ocho Rios, we had our first slight falling out. I made some comment about the depressing poverty everywhere around us on the island. On the bus transporting us around we had passed tumbledown shacks on every side, and we'd been told that the average income of Jamaican workers — those lucky enough to work at all, as the unemployment rate was incredibly high—was about two hundred dollars a year, while food prices generally were as high as or higher than in the States. But Amy disagreed with me, responding at once, softly and somewhat querulously, that she didn't see it that way at all; the people didn't seem all that poor to her, and after all, at least they didn't have to worry about property taxes, inflation, and things like that.

I quickly glanced around at her in surprise, unable to believe that she truly saw herself, with her fully furnished paid-for home, two paid-for cars, and Bob's monthly retirement pension, as poorer than the people here.

For a few minutes we really got into it quite hotly, Amy sticking to her position that poverty was relative, that she couldn't see that the Jamaicans were all that badly off, while I marveled that anyone living the relatively good life that Amy lived could feel that way. Then I quietly let the argument drop. Obviously Amy had felt miserably poor and unhappy all her life, and I guess if you feel that way it's not easy to see that others may be even worse off than you are.

We returned to the ship, had lunch, with Amy barely picking at her food, complaining that she felt uncomfortably full, what with all this garbage food she was eating, and then went to our cabin. The bay there at Ocho Rios was so lovely that I planned to go over to swim, but Amy, glasses on as she wrote some postcards, looked up and asked, like a child who has to get permission, if it was all right if she didn't go along. Would I mind very much? She didn't feel too well and would like to rest for a time.

Of course, I said, and with a smile and a kiss I left her there, while I went over to the bay to swim.

As things turned out, this was a grave error on my part. If I'd acted upset, acted as though she owed it to me to go with me, to please me at all times, to be "good" in every way, well, who knows? But I didn't want the kind of relationship in which I cracked the whip and Amy jumped, where I played the role of parent and made all the decisions while Amy tried to "earn" my love by being the ever-dutiful, ever-angelic child.

When I returned, Amy was sound asleep on the bed, face to the wall. I showered, dressed, then gently shook her awake to tell her it was time for dinner. Without rolling over to face me, she murmured that she didn't feel well, wasn't hungry, and did not plan to go to dinner; then she reclosed her eyes and fell back asleep.

My first meal without her.

After dinner when I returned to the cabin she was still sleeping, but in time she roused herself, said she felt better, showered, dressed, and went ashore with me to watch a native show being put on for the cruise passengers on the beach. She seemed to enjoy this, to be herself again, smiling at me, holding my hand, completely loving and sweet. I was relieved and delighted that she felt better.

But in the morning when I woke her for breakfast, her back to me, face turned to the wall, she again muttered that she didn't feel well, wasn't going to breakfast, and wasn't going on the tour for which we had already purchased tickets, in Port-au-Prince, Haiti, where we were now anchored. I'd have to take the tour by myself.

Which I did, and hated it. The poverty in Haiti made me see that Amy was right, the Jamaicans weren't really all that poor. Everywhere you turned in Haiti, or even without turning, simply sitting in the back of a cab waiting for traffic to move ahead, hands were stretched out toward you, black faces twisting in agony, dark eyes pleading with you for money, for food, for anything you might be willing to give. At every stop we made, all of us from the ship were immediately surrounded by frantic peddlers thrusting their factory-made trinkets into our hands, insisting that we buy. It was miserably hot and noisy and I couldn't wait for the tour to end, to get back to the ship and the comfort of our tiny cabin, and to Amy.

Amy was still sleeping when I got back, but this time she roused herself and sat huddled up against the headboard; when I asked her how she felt, she said, "Oh, I'm all right; as soon as we get home again I'll be fine," which sent my heart plummeting. This was Wednesday, only halfway through the cruise. If she planned to stay sick until we got home . . . oh, God.

Again she said, as I knew she was going to, that she wasn't hungry, wasn't coming to lunch. Again I offered to bring her anything she might want, but she waved me off. I'd already brought her various juice drinks, fresh fruit, anything I thought she might break down and take, but to no avail; the foods were simply sitting on our dresser, going to waste. Saying, "Don't worry about me, I'm all right," she lay down again full length, face to the wall, covering herself up, shutting me out. One full day.

I went to lunch myself, my third meal alone.

By then our waiter and our steward, as well as several passengers seated at nearby tables, asked me every time I appeared how my companion was, if she was still not feeling well. I answered their questions as courteously as possible, smiling, pretending I wasn't growing terribly lonely, terribly angry inside. If Amy planned to keep this up for the entire rest of the cruise —

When I returned to the cabin after lunch, Amy was gone. I located her sometime later up on one of the decks, lying face down on a bench. When I asked her how she felt, she murmured that she was better, the fresh air was doing her good. But then she immediately turned her face away, toward the back of the bench, again shutting me out.

So, nuts to you! I thought, and walked off, sighing, wondering how in the hell to deal with her.

I changed into my bathing suit, went for a swim in one of the pools, got to talking to a woman who was sunbathing alongside the pool, and had a reasonably enjoyable time. But what I should do about Amy was still nagging at me.

At five o'clock each day a Catholic service was offered, which, though not a Catholic, I had already attended twice, so again that evening, Wednesday, I attended. During the meditation period I tried very calmly to ask God what I should do, how to snap Amy out of it. If she continued on this way to the end of the cruise, it was hard to believe we would ever be close again. She would feel so ashamed and guilty, and I would feel so angry and disgusted, that we might never be able to work it through. So, please, God, I prayed, help me to reach some resolution now.

After formulating this prayer, I tried to become very quiet, very still, to allow answers to break through, and in almost no time I suddenly knew what I should do. Up to this point, so conditioned are we to treat physical illness as something for which the ill person is not responsible, I had been trying to act as sympathetic and helpful as possible, to give Amy all the emotional support I could. And this sure as hell hadn't done any good. Suddenly, as I sat there in the dim, restful quiet of the rolling bar-used-as-chapel, I knew that the proper tack to take was to act angry with her, blast at her with an anger that I did not truly feel.

When the service ended I returned to our cabin and quickly dressed for dinner, Amy again lying in our bunk, sleeping, face to the wall. But before I left I spoke to her, my voice curtly angry for the very first time.

"What?" Amy said, swinging half around to look at me, blinking her sleep-swollen eyes.

"I said," I repeated in a sharply hostile voice, "that I am now going to dinner, following which I'm going to the lounge show, and I don't know when the hell I'll be back."

Blinking at me, Amy said, as though in surprise, "Jane, you sound angry at me! Are you angry?"

"Well, my God, of course I'm angry!" I snapped. "What the hell do you expect?" With that I swung away and left, doing my damnedest to slam the door—but cabin doors don't really slam.

At dinner I was again given commiseration for the continuing poor health of my companion, but by that time I was sick of being commiserated with. I wanted company; this was my third meal alone for the day.

In the lounge I was asked to join three older women whom Amy and I had gotten to know slightly earlier in the cruise, and they all asked me how she was. When I explained that she was still feeling poorly, one of the women, Shirley, leaned over to say, "What's really bothering her, do you know?"

Shrugging, I said, "No, I don't. I'm sure she must be terribly angry at me for some reason, but why I don't know. It's easier for her to withdraw into illness than face me with what's really bugging her."

"So the hell with her," Shirley said. "Forget about her and enjoy yourself. What else can you do anyway? Though it's really a shame, the way she's wasting all the money she spent on this cruise."

"Yes," I said, thinking: The money *she* spent? But my momentary anger melted away as I again wondered how the hell to snap Amy out of whatever it was that she was going through.

When the lounge show came to an end, I returned somewhat reluctantly to the cabin. After showering, I crawled into bed beside Amy and, to my surprise, she rolled immediately onto her back, which wasn't exactly reaching out to me, but still it was better than having her face the wall, as she'd been doing for what seemed like forever. I lay in bed beside her, wondering whether I should make a move toward her, feeling angry, sad, and lonely by turns. In time the loneliness rolling through me became stronger than anything else and I reached over to touch her hand. In response she rolled over to face me.

"Amy, I've missed you," I said, and moved over to where I could kiss her.

After the kiss, she rolled onto her back again but I

moved over after her, kissing her several times on the mouth, then daring to touch her breasts. As my moves began to get really serious, Amy pushed me away, saying, "No, I didn't shower," which seemed to end that. But at least we'd begun to kiss and make up. I hoped.

In the morning, however, Amy again didn't feel well and wasn't going to breakfast; she rolled over to face the wall, again shutting me out. So much for our making up.

When I came back from another all-alone breakfast, I'd really had it; at that point I was more than ready to put into effect the advice I'd seemed to get during my meditation the preceding evening. Throwing myself on the bed, I grabbed hold of Amy, rolled her onto her back, and began forcefully kissing her, ordering her to get the hell out of bed and shower so that I could make love to her.

Taken by surprise, half laughing, half protesting, Amy kept demanding to know what was wrong with me, she'd never seen me like this before.

"Because you've never seen me angry before," I snarled, or tried hard to snarl; and I continued pressing down on her, kissing her, insisting that I was going to make love to her, while Amy struggled, protested, and demanded that I stop.

"I'm angry, goddammit!" I told her again.

Amy, struggling to sit up, to push me away, finally said, "Well, I'm angry too."

"So what are you angry about?" I asked, pulling away.

Her bleary, sleep-swollen eyes met mine, she bit at her lip, then finally dared to say, "Because you paid for the trip, which makes me feel so cheap and crumby."

"What?" I exploded, unable to believe what I'd heard.

"It just makes me feel so rotten, so cheap," Amy repeated, glancing away, then crawled to a sitting position to huddle up against the headboard.

"Well, my God, I can't believe it!" I cried. "If that's how you felt about it, you should have told me a month ago, when we made the reservations, not now. I didn't twist your arm to get you to come, you know. You came of your own free will."

"I know that," Amy agreed in a querulous voice, as her eyes flashed angrily over to meet mine. "But I didn't know I'd feel this way, and I can't help how I feel, you know."

"Maybe not," I snapped, "but you sure as hell can help how you act. And this is one hell of a way to act. All the money it cost to come—"

"So I'll pay you back," Amy broke in. "I'll pay you back every cent, I promise, the very first moment I can."

I looked at her steadily for quite some time, then broke into a broad grin. Leaning toward her, I said, "So pay me back right now. Go take a shower and come back to bed. That's the way you can pay me back, by letting me enjoy the rest of the cruise."

I managed to kiss her again, and after a moment of trying to pull away, Amy began kissing me back, her arms going around me. Before long she sighed and said, "All right, if you really want me to. Let go and I'll go shower."

Climbing off the bed, I told her that there was an important meeting I felt I should go to, one in which we would be given instructions for disembarking, but that I was sure it wouldn't take long and the moment it was over I'd be back and would expect to find her showered and undressed, waiting for me. Throwing her a good-bye kiss, I hurried out.

When I returned, about forty minutes later, Amy was sitting up in the bed, in a fresh pink nightgown, glasses on as she wrote some postcards. As I entered she greeted me with a bright, friendly smile. I took a quick shower, then joined her in bed. This time we really did kiss and make up, slapping a Bandaid over our continuing problem with money, in order to enjoy the rest of our cruise.

Ten

After making love we went to lunch together, the first time Amy had been in the dining room in two days. Though she mentioned that she'd better eat sparingly until her system got used to food again, she never again complained about not feeling well, and within a few hours she was her usual radiant self. And for the remainder of the cruise we had a marvelous time.

For me, of course, the most enjoyable part of the trip was simply being with Amy; it wouldn't have mattered where we were. I loved looking at her, talking with her, sharing a cabin with her. And the highlights of the trip for me were those frequent occasions when people we met openly expressed their admiration of Amy's astonishingly youthful beauty.

Of the three older women Amy and I had gotten to know aboard ship, two were in their early seventies, and the other, Shirley, was in her late sixties; all of them were widows. The evening I had attended the lounge show without Amy and joined them at their table, something had been said about husbands and I made a passing reference to Amy's husband.

Shirley immediately narrowed her eyes on me, almost angrily, and remarked quite sharply, "But Amy doesn't have a husband. Doris told me she doesn't." Shirley leaned across the table to say, "Doris, Amy doesn't have a husband, does she?"

Doris, a tiny, very active, feisty little woman of seventy-three, shook her head vigorously and said, "No, she doesn't have one."

Laughing, I said, "Well, I don't like to disagree, but she does have one."

Shirley eyed me closely. "She's living with her husband, you mean?"

"Oh, definitely."

"And you're married too?"

"Yes."

"And living with your husband?"

"Oh yes."

"Then—" I felt strongly that this wasn't what she really wanted to ask, but ordinary courtesy does insist upon some restraint, "how come you two are traveling together like this? Why aren't your husbands with you?"

"Because they are both very much stay-at-homes. Neither one can be pushed into going anywhere."

"Oh."

Shirley sat eyeing me closely again, to my very great pleasure. Having seen Amy and me together, I thought, she's perceptive enough to have caught on. She thought she had us all figured out: lesbian lovers, but now she's confused and can't figure it out.

"The four of you are very close, you mean?" Shirley suggested next, possibly trying to fit us into some kind of wife-swapping setup. Could Amy and I seem so close due to sharing of husbands?

"No, not exactly. Amy and I are very close, but the fact

is that our husbands didn't even meet until my husband drove us down to pick her up to go to the airport for this trip."

"Oh?" Shirley said, and lapsed back in her chair, obviously too perplexed to persevere in her questioning.

As the program ended a bit later and I got up to leave, commenting that I'd better return to the cabin to check on Amy, Shirley remarked dryly, "Yes, time to go check on your spouse," a remark I thoroughly enjoyed, despite my worry about my "spouse's" current withdrawal.

The next evening, after Amy and I had made up and she was back eating again, as we were leaving the dining room we were stopped by Doris, who caught hold of Amy's hand, and for several minutes we stood by their table, chatting with Shirley, Doris, and the third woman, Lucy. As though keener observation would somehow settle everything, Shirley stared fixedly across at Amy, possibly the first time she had looked really closely at her.

"Didn't you tell me," she asked me as Amy talked with Doris, "that your friend is a grandmother?"

"Yes," I answered, immediately pleased. "She's not only a grandmother, her grandchildren are teen-agers; the eldest one is fifteen years old."

"My God!" Shirley said, suitably impressed, I saw with delight, by what a miracle of beauty and agelessness Amy is.

"That woman's a grandmother," Shirley said to Lucy, seated beside her, who merely grunted, "Oh," sounding not in the least interested and even less impressed.

"Amy," Shirley said a moment later, raising her voice to interrupt the conversation Amy and Doris were having, "I just have to mention that you're the youngest-looking grandmother I've ever seen."

"Why, thank you," Amy said in surprise, blue eyes sparkling, smooth skin glowing, looking twelve years old. "You've made my day."

During our trip two people asked if I was Amy's

mother—one, a young Jamaican boy trying to sell us some souvenirs, the other an elderly woman we had met aboard ship.

"Oh no," Amy said quickly in response to the elderly woman, her cheeks flushing with embarrassment.

"You mean you're just friends?" the woman persisted. Possibly she had seen us at some time enjoyably engrossed in each other and couldn't figure it out.

"Oh, more than friends," Amy protested, still flustered.

"Sisters?"

Amy peeked hurriedly around at me, as though wondering whether she should lie, but then, blushing even more, she said, "No, not sisters."

"Well, if you're not sisters, how can you be even closer than friends?"

"Very *good* friends," I threw in, catching the woman's eye and shutting her up.

In Nassau, instead of taking the regularly scheduled tour we went off on our own to visit a yoga ashram on Paradise Isle. Two American women we met there, who welcomed us in the friendliest fashion, soon asked if Amy was a movie star.

"Who, me?" Amy responded in surprise. "Heavens, no, I'm only a housewife."

"But you look just like a movie star!" the woman persisted, staring at her. "Surely she is one?" she said to me.

"No," I said, grinning. "She's beautiful enough to be one, but she isn't one."

"It's all this makeup I wear," Amy whispered to me as we walked away. "That's what fooled her. People figure that anyone who'd wear all this goo just has to be an actress or something like that."

Laughing, I said, "I don't think it's that at all. A lot of women wear makeup, many of them a lot more than you wear, but they're not mistaken for movie stars. And you apply it so expertly that it's not all that easy to see that you're wearing it. I think it's partly the great way you walk, as though you own the world, and partly, of course, because you're so beautiful."

"Oh, sure," Amy mocked. "With all the stuff that comes out of jars I'm beautiful. When I get up in the morning I look like hell."

"Don't give me that line anymore," I said. "I've seen you when you get up, and you look good to me."

During our days aboard ship Amy had gotten to where she could face me fully, talk with me, laugh with me, be herself, before she settled down in front of the mirror to make up her face. This alone, for me, made the trip worth the price.

After I'd said this, Amy grinned, and we walked along hand in hand, as we often did, two women in love.

That afternoon, as we were walking back to the ship after a stroll through downtown Nassau, Amy suggested that we shoot the last of her film. She took a snap of me standing in front of the cruise ship, then I took one of her. As Amy was posing, a slender, attractive, middle-aged man came walking back toward the ships. Not only our ship was moored there, so was our sister ship.

Eyeing Amy hungrily, the man inquired politely, "Are you on the *Starward* or *Skyward*?"

"The *Starward*," Amy answered gaily, smiling. The picture now taken, she began walking toward me.

The man swung around to watch her with a long, hungry stare. "Wish I were," he muttered wistfully, then with a sigh he walked on, sadly shaking his head.

Reaching me, grinning, Amy took the camera from me and said, "Why didn't you go to that man and say, 'Leave her alone, she's mine'?"

The highlight of my trip.

For all Amy's talk of how her physical attractiveness comes straight out of tubes and jars, it isn't the eye shadow, mascara, powder, or pale lipstick she uses that make her beautiful; it's the warmth and trust sparkling in her deep blue eyes, the radiant glow of her unblemished skin, the soft curves of her perfectly formed mouth, and her brilliant, childlike smile.

People take one look at her and know that she could never be mean, spiteful, or unsympathetic, that she doesn't have it in her to be petty, greedy, or vindictive. Somehow she has moved through the world, for half a century, without in any way being corrupted by life; or, as my mother put it on meeting her, "She still hasn't lost her innocence." On occasion, when the child momentarily disappears, she can seem infinitely saddened by life, in deep despair over what she has seen, but never corrupted by it.

Amy is beautiful on the outside for one reason only: because she is so sweet and beautiful within.

I had worried beforehand that we might find seven days sharing a small cabin just too much togetherness, that small irritations and frustrations might arise, but, apart from Amy's illness and her withdrawal over the money issue, we sailed through our week at sea without a ripple, then had our first falling out, as minor as it was, after disembarking.

As we were going through customs, piling our cases onto the table and having them pushed through, a porter began grabbing them up and putting them on his dolly. While we were not terribly overburdened, nevertheless, with our various purchases, souvenirs, etcetera, we had more cases and packages than we could carry, so I was happy to see what the porter was doing, but Amy, by my side, apparently wasn't.

"What are you doing?" she demanded of the porter, with some irritation in her usually soft, ladylike voice. "Put those back down!"

"You can't just let them pile up, lady," the porter answered nonchalantly, grabbing up more of our cases. "Others are behind, waiting to get through."

"Don't worry, we'll manage, just put those back down!" Amy ordered again.

Again the porter ignored her. By this time he had everything on his dolly except for an overnight case Amy had grabbed up and was furiously clutching. Being questioned by the customs official, I only took in what was happening with the porter peripherally, and the next thing I knew we were through customs, crossing a street, and coming to rest by a rent-a-car sign. I indicated to the porter that this was where we wanted to be, he unloaded our bags, and I opened my purse and handed him two dollars.

"How much did you give him?" Amy asked after he'd walked away.

"A couple of dollars," I murmured, concerned with other things, not yet aware that a storm was brewing. "Why?"

"That was too much," Amy complained. "That was throwing money away."

I smiled, touching her arm, trying to smooth it all over. "But not much. And I didn't have any quarters left."

"A dollar would have been plenty," Amy said, sounding even more angry.

"Well, the guide on tipping says a quarter per bag," I defended myself, "so with six bags —"

"Five," Amy snapped. "I carried this one." She gave a kick at her carry-on case.

"Okay, so I'm sorry. I wonder how soon the agent for the rental cars will get here."

We discussed this for a minute or two, then Amy said, softening, "I'm sorry about the fuss I raised about that porter, but you did overtip him."

Reaching out to touch her arm again, grinning, madly in love, I said, "So, I'm sorry. Will you forgive me?"

Dimpling, Amy said, "Probably not. You'll probably never hear the end of it. A year from now, five years from now, ten years from now —"

"I know, I know," I said, laughing.

"Every time we go anywhere, every time I see you tipping anyone, I'll throw it at you again: 'Remember that porter in Miami you overtipped?' "

"I was just thinking that if it's going to be a problem, next time we go anywhere, you carry all the money and tip as you please, and I'll just look the other way."

"Well, you did tip him too much," Amy reiterated.

Then the man from the car-rental agency showed up. We learned that since we had not reserved a car we'd have to go to the airport to get one; the bus to the airport was parked across another narrow street. The first thing we knew, as we began lifting our bags the same porter who had moved us to this spot showed up again and began loading our bags onto his dolly, another one-minute moving job. As he put our bags down alongside the bus, I opened my purse again, and this time I gave him only a dollar.

As we climbed into the bus and took our seats, Amy's lips pressed together in disapproval. "You tipped him again," she said accusingly as I took my seat beside her.

"Well—" At that point I really did feel I was being persecuted. Wasn't one supposed to tip? And considering that we'd just spent close to two thousand dollars for our week's trip, what the hell was all this fuss about a measly three dollars, total, in tips?

"He didn't even expect it," Amy added angrily, glaring at me. "My God, you'd already overtipped him for carrying our bags a lousy twenty feet, then he takes them another twenty feet and you tip him again! Can't you see that that's just throwing money around?"

Under her withering glare I could only shrug, not knowing how to attempt further defense for what was apparently in her eyes an indefensible action. "I guess I'll never hear the end of this," I muttered.

"I guess not," Amy said, but after a minute she softened and reached out to take my hand. "I told you I can get really bitchy at times," she said. "I'm sorry."

"Don't be," I said, squeezing the soft hand I held. "It makes me feel very married." Which it did.

Amy broke into a warm, happy grin and we sat there smiling at each other for all the world to see how we felt. Two crazy people in love. Two people crazy in love.

We had already checked our bags through on our afternoon flight, rented a car, and were off for a few hours' driving tour of Miami, before I suddenly took in the lousy thing I'd done in tipping that man.

I faced Amy and said, "Amy, it just hit me what I did in tipping that porter, and, sweetheart, I'm sorry. I heard you tell him to put our bags back down —"

"We didn't ask him to take them," Amy broke in, "he just started piling them up all on his own, which he had no right to do."

"Right," I said. "And since I heard you tell him to knock it off, the last thing I should have done was tip him. I should have told him to go to hell. To tip him was disloyal of me and I had no business doing it. You were completely in the right, I was wrong, and I'm sorry. Will you forgive me?"

Amy gave me a meltingly loving glance as I reached over to take her hand. Squeezing my hand, she said, "Better watch it, or we'll wind up renting a motel room."

I burst out laughing. "I know, I've already thought of that, but it seems a bit extravagant when we've just had a week together on the ship."

We spent a lovely few hours sightseeing in Miami Beach, sat for a time on the beach watching the ocean and talking, then that afternoon returned to the airport to fly back to our husbands and separate homes.

But I felt so close to Amy by then that it no longer seemed to matter that we didn't, for now couldn't, live together. After our week away I felt so solidly married to her I knew that nothing could ever part us again.

Eleven

I saw Amy once after our trip, on a Monday evening, then she stopped answering her phone, and when I was finally able to reach her, on Christmas Day, she told me that we were through. And when I sent her a letter asking if we could meet to discuss the situation, she mailed the letter back to me unopened, unread. Once again my beautiful doll was fearfully bolting away.

For me, in spite of all my pretrip worries, the transition at home couldn't have been smoother. When we arrived in Los Angeles we were met at the airport not only by Russ and Tommy but by my mother, a married brother and his wife, and two of their children. After the initial greetings, Tommy cornered me and walked by my side as we went for our luggage, excitedly telling me what had happened while I was away. His PSAT results had arrived; he had posted the highest score in his school, and in fact had gotten the highest score on the English section ever achieved by any student in the school.

After we'd gotten our luggage, I walked alongside Russ to the parking lot. He caught me up on other things that had happened while I was away, and by the time we were all piling into my brother's station wagon, it was almost as though I'd never been away—except for the memories I had.

From my brother's house, the four of us, Amy and I, Russ and Tommy, drove the rest of the way home in our car. Tommy, now sixteen, was driving, Russ was beside him in the front seat, and Amy and I were in the back. As we drove along the freeway Amy reached over to hold my hand, and I glanced around at her, smiling, loving her with all my heart and feeling that she was so much a part of me now, so inseparably my love, that it didn't matter that very soon we would part. Not for a single moment did I experience the depression I had briefly suffered following our weekend "honeymoon" trip.

But the transition for Amy apparently didn't go nearly as smoothly, and, for the second time after a trip, my sweet darling panicked and ran away.

We returned home on Saturday evening, the week before Christmas. When I phoned Amy the following day, around two in the afternoon, she was warmly, sweetly loving. Bob, who had gone on a hunting trip during our absence, had returned home a couple of hours before, and, while naturally very tired, he seemed fine. We made a luncheon date for the following day.

Around eleven Monday morning Amy phoned to say that something had unexpectedly come up and she wouldn't be able to keep our date. She didn't say what the problem was, but that was typical of her.

"Bob isn't sick?" I countered, immediately worried, but she assured me it wasn't that, nor was she sick.

"It's just something that's come up," she explained, without explaining. "I know you'll be over at Russ's office all day tomorrow, but maybe we could make it Wednesday?"

"Maybe," I murmured, my pulse suddenly racing with

a new idea. Not precisely a new idea, actually something I'd been thinking about for months but so far had not gotten around to suggesting. "Amy, if you're tied up during the day today, how about tonight? Are you free?"

"Well, maybe. What do you have in mind?"

"The lesbian rap session in Garden Grove. You remember, I told you about going down there. I've thought for a long time that I'd really love going down there with you. How about it? Would you even consider going?"

After only the briefest hesitation Amy said, "All right, sure. What time?"

"From about eight to ten. I'll pick you up about seven-twenty, all right?"

"Fine," Amy said. "See you then. Now I really have to run. I love you, Jane."

"And I love you."

As we hung up my heart was singing. I felt so excited I wanted to run outside and shout out the news: Amy and I, my love and I, would be appearing in public together, in a gay group, as a lesbian couple, for the very first time.

Though we had often appeared in public together before, of course, at the various restaurants where we lunched, in the park where we often sat for hours on the grass talking, on our trips, and while on occasion we walked hand in hand down the street or kissed good-bye in public view, short of wearing signs on our backs, HEY, WE'RE LOVERS! or shouting the news to passersby, we were for the most part invisible as almost everyone is in even a medium-sized city; no one paid us the least mind, no one seemed to notice or care who we were, what we were, or how we felt about each other, any more than we paid attention to how those we passed anonymously on the street were thinking or feeling. But now, tonight, in a rap session . . .

At last we'd be able to shed our anonymity, if only for a couple of hours, and openly be in company what we were in private: two women in love with each other.

I could hardly wait.

When I picked Amy up that evening, she had never looked more adorable; she wore a blue sweater and blue jeans and carried a blue windbreaker jacket. Climbing into my car, she flashed me a happy, childlike grin, reached over to take my hand, and said, "Hi. It's been so long, I've missed you."

"And I've missed you." We laughed and kissed and I felt so goddamn happy I could almost have died of it.

There were fourteen women at the rap session that night, ranging in age from about nineteen to one woman who was possibly a year or two older than Amy and I. On the drive down I'd asked Amy whether she cared if others there knew that we were a couple; if she'd prefer that no one knew, we could walk in separately and I'd be very careful not to give anything away.

"But why?" Amy protested. "I love you, and I couldn't care less who knows."

"You're sure?"

"Of course I'm sure."

The rap group that night was even more congenial and good-natured than usual, or maybe it only seemed that way because I felt so keyed up and happy. In going around the room to introduce ourselves, we were told to say a word or two about how we had spent the preceding week. It was Amy's turn before it was mine, and with a delightful blush she said, "I'm Amy, and I spent last week on a cruise with Jane," her eyes sliding around to me so that everyone would know whom she meant.

Her comment elicited immediate exclamations of surprise, envy and delight, and during a brief question-and-answer period Amy explained that the Caribbean cruise had been our first one and that we'd had a wonderful time. When the conversational ball was at last handed on to me, I had little to add except, "Well, I'm Jane and I spent last week on a cruise with Amy," which brought a round of appreciative laughter. How my ego lapped it up! And my soul expanded with love to where I wanted to embrace the entire universe. How sweet life was.

As the session was drawing to a close, the facilitator remarked that she planned to adjourn to the gay club a few blocks away and would be happy to be joined there by anyone who wished to go. As we were walking out, I asked Amy if she'd drop by the club just for a dance or two.

"Oh, I don't know, Jane," she said, frowning. "You know how I hate bars, all that smoking and drinking. But, well, all right, just for a dance or two." She affectionately squeezed my hand.

Ten or eleven of us from the rap were soon gathered around a table at the bar, where there was a small dance floor and a juke box. Amy and I each ordered a glass of orange juice, then we danced, the first time we had ever danced together in public, and I greatly enjoyed it. After we returned to our table, another woman asked Amy to dance, and after a slight hesitation she accepted. Then I asked the woman sitting beside me if she'd care to dance, she accepted, and I had one fantastic time. I was riding the crest, with no idea that the wave would soon crash.

After a few more dances Amy excused herself to go to the ladies' room. A moment later a hard, thin hand clasped down on my shoulder. In surprise, I glanced around to find myself staring into a furiously scowling face—that of Frances, the woman I'd spent a couple of hours with here in the bar following a rap session just about the time I'd had my first luncheon date with Amy; Frances was the one who'd spat at me in fury that night that she didn't dig married women.

"Well, look who's come back," Frances said sarcastically, blowing moist beer fumes into my face; it was easy to see that she was a slight bit to leeward. "You've got your nerve, you two-timing bitch. You know what really pisses me off about a woman like you? You want it all, the security and respectability of marriage, while you play around on the side. You want to have your cake and eat it too—that's what pisses me off. So, married woman, fuck you!"

Frances straightened up, her hand released its angry grip on my shoulder, she gave me the finger, then unsteadily strode off.

"Well," the woman sitting next to me said with a little laugh, letting out her breath. She opened her mouth to say something, then shut it again.

"Yes, I'm married," I said.

"Living with your husband, you mean?"

"Yes, living with my husband."

"And he's gay too?"

Sighing, I said, "No, he's straight, whatever that means. That is, he doesn't have any conscious desire to make love to another man."

"Wow." A momentary silence while the woman took a gulp of her beer, then her eyes lifted to meet mine again. "And he knows about you?"

"Yes."

"And—your girl friend, does she know about your husband?"

"Oh yes."

The woman laughed again. Her elbow nudged mine, and her cheeks were flushed. "I've got a friend—gay—who lives with her girl friend and the girl friend's boyfriend, and the three of them get it on together, all three of them. From what I hear, there's quite a bit of that these days."

Feeling sad and somehow dirty, I said, "Well, the three of us don't. It's not like that." Physically/sexually it wasn't, but on some other level—? Was it fair, loving, or decent to want it all? Not only to want it all but to have it all? Poor lonely, angry Frances, wasn't her lifestyle better, more honest than mine? Did anyone ever have a right to it all?

When Amy came back she suggested we leave, which at that point I was glad to do. In the car she asked me who the woman was who'd grabbed me by the shoulder and spoken to me in such an obviously unfriendly fashion.

"How'd you know about that? I thought you'd gone to the restroom."

She had, but it had been occupied, and while she'd waited in the hallway outside she'd had an unobstructed view of the table where I was sitting and had seen Frances come over to tell me off.

"Oh, it was a woman I met a long time ago at one of the sessions, just about the time I met you, and she's furious at me for being married and wanting a woman lover too. That's 'wanting to have my cake and eat it too.' "

Amy sighed. "I know. I've thought of that, and in a way it just doesn't seem right, does it?"

"It feels right to me," I said, though at that moment I wasn't all that sure. Was I being unconscionably greedy? Even though I couldn't see that I was hurting anyone, were we supposed to deliberately restrict, confine our lives, our loves, our selves? Did God demand that we enforce such limits, or were we confined and restricted solely by our own uncertainties and fears? If God was joy, and we were here on earth to somehow come closer to Him, could those things in which we took incredible joy be wrong?

We drove in disheartened silence for a while; then Amy said in a soft little voice, "Sometimes I feel so disloyal; after all, I do have a husband."

Then silence again, mile after mile.

Feeling cold, I switched on the heater, and our sadness was orchestrated by the dismal noise of the fan blowing drying warmth into the car. Should we scurry back into our separate lives for fear of what we might be doing to our immortal souls?

When I pulled into Amy's driveway, for the first time she didn't turn to me with a sweet smile, ready to say goodnight with a hug and a kiss. Instead, she climbed right out, walked around the back of the car, and stopped by my door. By then I had the window rolled down and could see her face in the reflected light of the headlamps.

"Don't worry about me," I said. "Do whatever you think is best for you."

"You're sweet." She leaned down to kiss me goodnight, whispered, "I love you," then broke into a little run to the side door of her house. I waited until she was safely inside, then drove home. After our week's trip, so perfect in and for itself, to come back feeling so in love, so married—well, no matter what came next, there was no way I wouldn't feel eternally grateful for the joy we had already shared.

What happened next was that Amy stopped answering her phone. I called her on Tuesday, then Wednesday, then Thursday, trying a dozen times each day, but there was no answer. I knew that Bob, who spent much of his time out in their backyard, rarely bothered to answer the phone, but always before, if I tried two or three times during the day, I'd been able to reach Amy.

Thursday evening I was in Russ's bedroom, talking with him, when he asked me what was troubling me; I seemed very blue. On impulse, I confided that I hadn't talked to Amy since Monday, hadn't been able to reach her by phone, and didn't know what was going on.

"Go phone her," Russ ordered. "There's no point in going on like this. Anything's better than uncertainty."

Realizing that he was right, I walked resolutely out to the kitchen and dialed Amy's number. I'd rarely phoned her this late at night—it was just before nine—because I didn't want to intrude upon time that I felt belonged to Bob.

This time she picked up the phone on the third ring and murmured hello.

"Amy! How are you? I can't believe I've finally reached you."

"Oh, have you tried before?"—sounding dismal and distant. "When?"

"When *haven't* I? Are you all right?"

"Oh yes, I'm fine. And Bob's fine too."

Feeling tense, angry, sick at heart, I leaned against the sink and stared down at the green tile floor. "Well, what have you been up to, anyway?" No response. "I've missed you." Again, no response. Working up my nerve, knowing what the answer would be, I said, "How about lunch with me tomorrow?"

"Oh, I don't think so," she answered, this time sounding not quite so distant.

"You can't make it?"

"No. Sorry, but I can't."

At that I exploded. "All right, Amy, for God's sake, what's happening? You must know I've been trying for days to get in touch with you. Since you were gone so much, why didn't you phone me sometime when you were home? The very last thing you said to me, last Monday night, was that you love me. What kind of love is this?"

No answer for an appreciable time, then she murmured that she hadn't been feeling well. "But I'm all right now," she added quickly. "And, Jane, I just have to go now. I'm sorry, but I have to." She hung up.

Well, goddammit anyway, I thought, and slammed down my receiver, hot tears threatening to flood my eyes. Why was Amy kicking me out?

Two days later, Christmas Day, I called Amy again. This time she answered the phone at once, sounding happy and cheerful. "Good-morning, merry Christmas!"

"Merry Christmas to you," I said. "I hope you and Bob have a very happy one."

"Oh, it's you"—voice already beginning to fade.

"Yes, it's me. You sound as though you're feeling better. Are you?"

"I told you I was feeling all right," she responded, with just a hint of irritation in her fading-away voice.

I struggled to make conversation for another minute or two, telling her what I'd been up to, that I missed her, that Tommy and I were going to my mother's for the day for a big family gathering, with Russ staying home, as usual, while Amy murmured an occasional, completely uninterested "Oh." Growing more and more exasperated, I finally said, straight out, "Okay, Amy, level with me. Have you decided again that you're through with me? Are you breaking off?"

A long silence, then a faraway "Well . . ."

"Well?" I challenged, momentarily feeling more annoyed than anything else.

Still no further comment from Amy, just a long, nerve-racking silence. "Oh, for God's sake, Amy!" I snapped. "After all this time, don't I at least deserve an honest answer? Have you decided again that you're through with me?"

"Well . . ." said so softly, sounding so far away, that I could barely hear, "you did tell me to do whatever I felt was best for me, and —"

"And the best thing you can think of is to break up with me, is that what you're saying?" No comment. "Can you tell me why?" No comment. "Oh, come on now, if you're breaking off, at least get up the nerve to put it into words!"

Another long silence, then Amy's terribly faraway voice: "All right. Yes, I have decided that we're through."

"Goddammit," I said; then I added angrily, pettily, "You might at least have decided this before we went on the cruise," a comment that I immediately regretted and for which I later apologized.

But for the moment it helped, sparking Amy into a semblance of life. "I told you I'd pay you back for that," she said quickly, in a voice I could now hear. "And I will."

"Fine," I said, no longer angry, feeling guilty instead over the cheap crack I'd made, which did not at all reflect how I felt; no matter what happened from here on out, I wouldn't for anything give up our week together. "When?"

"Well—" Amy laughed. "You know I don't have the money right now, but I'll pay you back the moment I can."

"But I don't want to wait," I said. "I'm not willing to wait. Either you pay me back right now or I'll be another Shylock and come down there and pay myself back by slashing off a pound of your flesh."

"Oh, you will?" she countered, and laughed even harder, sounding thoroughly delighted.

Our conversation then veered to serious again, Amy insisting softly that the best thing for me to do was forget her, our affair had been a mistake, please just forget the whole thing. We exchanged holiday greetings again, several times wished each other the best, then both hung up. Amy's Christmas gift to me.

I felt depressed for possibly two minutes after the call, then my spirits bounced back. If Amy meant it this time . . . But I felt sure she didn't. She had not even tried to claim that she no longer loved me; she was just feeling frightened and guilty again. Somehow we'd work things out. Besides, today was Christmas, a day to relax and enjoy oneself.

The following Monday evening I decided, on impulse, to go down to the rap session in Garden Grove again, drawn, as were so many others, to a place where women could voice their lesbian worries and be assured of a sympathetic audience. But could I be so assured? If I leveled with the group, "Hey, I'm married and my lover is married but still we've been getting it on together too," how much sympathy would I get?

Probably about as much as I deserved.

Driving down to the rap I was in a reasonably calm and philosophic mood, not unduly upset, in fact feeling much happier about Amy than I had during the frustrating days of the preceding week, during which I had unsuccessfully tried to contact her. So, once again she was through with me. Well, if she really meant it this time, I still felt grateful for all we'd shared.

Could she possibly be right that we should break up?

When I entered the rap room I was greeted with a couple of questions as to why Amy wasn't with me, which I fielded in friendly, evasive fashion, immediately glad that I'd decided to come, grateful that there was a place where a woman like me could go to feel relaxed and to express herself freely. Even if I spread the whole truth out before this group, I suddenly felt, I'd be offered, at least from most of those present, genuine sympathy and support. I felt this strongly, and was instantly fond of every woman there. Each one had been through too much trauma herself, had had to put up with too much unpleasant prejudice, to prejudge me. I sank down on one of the sofas, feeling happy and at peace.

The next woman to come through the door was one I'd met almost a year before at one of the raps and still hadn't forgotten: Claire, who had told me that she'd been married for years but that after her children were grown and gone she and her husband had split up and she'd come out in the gay world. The moment she entered I smiled in joyful recognition; noticing me, she smiled back and came over to sit beside me.

"Well, hello. Haven't seen you here in a long time."

"I was here last week," I countered, "at which time I didn't see you."

"No, I missed last week. Anyway, how have you been? The last time I saw you you'd just had a luncheon date with a pretty blond woman who was married. How did that work out?"

I burst out laughing. "Fantastically." I remembered my Christmas Day conversation with Amy. "Though at the moment things don't look all that good."

"I'd love to hear all about it," Claire said. "Maybe we could get together after the rap for a drink or something."

"Fine, it's a date," I said, feeling wonderfully glad that I'd come.

As the rap broke up, Claire and I decided against going to the nearby gay bar; it would be easier to talk somewhere else. We met at a restaurant a couple of miles up the road, took a booth, and began spilling out all the details of our private lives. Claire had gotten involved with two women in the months since I'd seen her last, but neither relationship was very satisfying to her. I told her all about my affair with Amy, including the fact that it was currently in the *off* position.

"Though I'm not really very worried," I told Claire. "I can understand what Amy's going through right now and I really and truly sympathize with her. After all, I had three or four years to prepare myself emotionally for what I planned to get into, and she had no real preparation at all. When we first met, I thought it was absolutely fantastic the way she could be so accepting of everything. I think there are bound to be times when she has to stand off and wonder and worry about what she's gotten into and where it will lead. And it makes perfect sense that it would happen right now. We had this nearly perfect week together, come home feeling more in love than ever, it was sure to hit her sometime that what she's gotten into isn't just child's play, it's dynamite. So she's drawn back from me and needs time to work it through."

"But what if she works it through," Claire suggested, "in a way that completely eliminates you? What if she decides that from now on she's going to fall back into the role of faithful, devoted wife and never let her affections stray again?"

"Well, if that's the way it works out, that's the way it works out." I shrugged. "I don't think it will come to that, but it won't destroy me if it does. I know she loves me, in fact that's the root of the problem. The more she faces how important I am to her, that in many ways I've become the core, the center of her life, the more it frightens her, so she has to run for cover, at least temporarily. But no matter what happens from this point on, I'm happy and grateful for everything. Period."

"Great," Claire said, grinning at me. "Wish I could say the same."

Following this we returned to a discussion of the frantic upheavals in her romantic life, which would make a book in itself.

The next day I wrote Amy a brief letter asking if we could get together someday, possibly for lunch, to discuss our situation; that I didn't like to think of her trembling in fear that I might carry out my threat to come slash off a pound of her flesh; that I had said that only in anger and had not meant it. I also said—like many another discarded lover—that I didn't see why we couldn't still be friends even if she no longer wanted to be physically intimate. I still loved her very much, would always feel concerned about her, and was ready to make whatever compromises were necessary for her to feel comfortable again with me.

That was on Tuesday. On Friday, the last day of the year, I received an answer, an envelope addressed by Amy and with her return address on it. Trembling with both fear and excitement, I ripped open the envelope, and out fell my letter to her, still sealed in its envelope. Also, the passbook to our joint account, in which we'd left twenty dollars to keep it open. Nothing else. No little note from Amy, just the passbook and my unopened, unread letter. An eloquent answer, surely answer enough.

Thinking, Well, dammit anyway! I marched straight to the phone and called Amy and when she answered I said, "Hey, you hard-hearted bitch, what the hell is this? I send you a nice, sweet, loving letter, and you won't even read it? You say you love me. What kind of love is this?"

"Oh, Jane, that's just it," Amy said, moaning softly. "I knew that's the kind of letter it would be, sweet and loving, that's why I couldn't bear to read it. You told me to do whatever seemed best for me, but now you don't want me to. That's not fair."

"It *is* fair," I yelled, "because the thing that's best for you is me, and the sooner you realize that, the better it'll be for both of us."

"Says who?" Amy countered, laughing.

"I do. Didn't you just hear me? Even if you don't love me anymore, we're still friends, aren't we? And what kind of friend would do a thing like this?"

"But I didn't say I don't still love you," she said, in a firmer, clearer voice. "I do still love you, but at the same time I feel . . ."

"What?"

"Oh, Jane, you know."

"No, I don't. Tell me again. You love me but still you feel . . ."

Laughter was bubbling richly in both our voices, and we were falling into a familiar pattern of playful argument. Before long I said, "Well, yoga class resumes Monday night, you know. Are you planning to go?"

"Well—" followed by a long pause.

"I'll pick you up at the usual time, all right?"

"Well—"

"Oh, come on, Amy, you know you don't want to drop out of class, and as long as your house is right on my way, why shouldn't I pick you up? I'm still me, you know, and I'm not going to bite you."

"Sometimes I almost wish you would," Amy said, half annoyed, half laughing. "If you weren't always so sweet and loving . . ."

On Monday Amy said she didn't feel well enough to go to class that night, but on Wednesday night I picked her up at the usual time, after class we stopped for something to eat, and then, after I'd driven her home, we sat in my car talking, and soon were embracing and kissing each other. Before many days had passed she came to my home early one afternoon, and once again we dove joyfully into bed.

Twelve

After our weekend trip to the mountains Amy mentioned occasionally that she had to find a job. Though for the most part she resolutely refused to discuss with me her financial situation, I gathered that the primary reason she felt the need to work was to earn money for the things she wanted, especially new carpeting for her home, and not because she and Bob couldn't meet their everyday expenses.

Whenever Amy talked about getting a job, it depressed me. I'd point out to her that each of us has only so many hours per week, also only so much energy, and Amy, though generally in good health in the sense of being free from pain or disease, was far from robust; rather, as I'd learned from our trips together, she was somewhat frail, tired easily, and didn't have anywhere near the reserves of energy that I did. In fact, Amy commented frequently to me, rather wistfully, "Jane, you just never tire, do you?" Of course I did; I just didn't tire anywhere near as quickly as she did.

"If you go to work, we won't get to see much of each other," I would argue with her. "Keeping house on top of having a job . . . Dammit, Amy, even with the best will in the world, you simply wouldn't have the time or energy to crowd me in!"

Eyes sparkling with tears, she would say softly, "But, Jane, I really don't have any choice. We're simply not making it." Which would start us off on another argument, because I felt she did have a choice. All she had to do was unbend a bit and agree to take money from me.

Although Amy occasionally made these comments about having to go to work, for months she did nothing about it, first saying that she wanted to wait until the weather was cooler. Going through the menopause, she was bothered with almost continual hot flashes. Then as fall slowly gave way to winter, she said she'd decided to wait until after the holidays. Then in January she decided to wait until our yoga class ended at the end of the month. By this time I had been lulled into a false feeling of safety, an underlying, never-expressed belief that when it came to finding a job she was all talk and no action, that she would always find some excuse to postpone the dreaded day when she'd actually go out looking. The very day after our yoga class ended, however, she proved me wrong.

She began going out almost every weekday trying to find a job, putting in applications everywhere she thought there was the least possibility that she might be hired, which upset me terribly. But when I tried to argue her out of what she was doing, I got nowhere. When I pointed out again that if she found full-time work she simply wouldn't have time to squeeze me into her life anymore, she smiled sweetly and replied that one, she wouldn't be working forever, and two, she was hoping to find a part-time job. When I continued to complain even about this, she told me very lovingly that in order to please me, to keep her daytime hours free so that we could continue to see each other, she hoped to find a nighttime job, which would mean she'd be working during the hours she normally spent at home with Bob, not the hours she spent with me.

Instead of making me feel better, this made me feel even more depressed and selfish as hell. Amy would be out somewhere slaving away, growing more and more tired, getting closer to the point of utter exhaustion, for a lousy two and a half or three bucks an hour. In order to have free time in the afternoons to spend with Amy, I customarily began working at seven in the morning, clearing up paperwork from the office while Russ ate his breakfast and read the morning paper, and on occasion I worked until nine or ten at night, but I felt I stayed well within my limits and never risked losing my enjoyment of life; however, I just didn't feel that this would be true for Amy.

I worried and stewed about this all during February, wishing to hell that I had someone with whom I could discuss it. Although I normally talk over every problem I face with someone, my mother, my husband, or a friend, there was no one with whom I felt I could discuss this. I shied away from discussing it with Russ, unsure as to how he would react to my offering Amy money. Whereas I tend to feel rich no matter how little I have — I have always felt greatly blessed by God, almost embarrassingly fortunate — Russ, like Amy, tends to feel poor no matter how much he has. So I didn't want to risk having him blow up and begin laying down the law about what I could do financially and what I couldn't. I didn't feel free to discuss the problem with my mother, either. One day months before, I'd tried to tell her about Amy, that Amy and I had become lovers, but as I steered the conversation that way, she immediately steered it away again, as though determined not to hear me say it, so I'd let the subject drop; therefore, I doubted that she would feel comfortable if I tried to discuss with her what was upsetting me now.

Of course, I had several friends who knew all about my affair with Amy, but they also knew Amy personally, and I knew damn well that Amy wouldn't like it one bit if I discussed it with them; and the same held true for the women we'd gotten to know at the lesbian raps in Garden Grove. Amy felt that her financial situation was her own business and no one else's. She wouldn't even discuss it with me, so how could I go around blabbing about it to my friends?

But I needed to discuss it with someone, to voice my complaints, to air my very real doubts and worries. In urging money on Amy, was I trying to reduce her to dependency on me, to rob her of her self-respect? Was she right in refusing to accept a penny from me, even if it meant having to go to work, which she so obviously didn't want to do?

I didn't know, couldn't decide. All I was certain of was that from the time we'd met, Amy had been sending out double signals when it came to money, to the gifts I gave her, and to the trips we took. On the one hand, she always claimed that she didn't feel right about taking things from me; on the other, she never seemed so pleased, loving and sweet, as when she gave in and accepted something from me.

I had always felt very strong, very able to take care of myself. At the same time, I had always felt very loved, very sure that there were people who would step in and take care of me if I couldn't take care of myself. Amy seemed to depend solely on herself, to be afraid to trust anyone but herself. That seemed to me a lonely and basically unhappy way to be. I wanted her to see that she could trust others.

I didn't know, however, whether this could be achieved or whether I was going about it the right way. And Amy continued to look for work all that month.

I repeatedly suggested, in all seriousness, that if she simply had to go to work, instead of going to work for a stranger, at hard labor she wouldn't enjoy, she could work for me, easy work that she would enjoy. I'd hire her to lunch with me, attend raps, spend time with me in bed, for which I would pay her two hundred dollars a month. Amy would laugh and remind me sweetly that she was already doing all that for free—and then she would go right on spending hours each week looking for work, wasting gas, putting wear and tear on her car. The job market was very tight and no one wanted to hire her—except for me.

In March Amy gave up trying, apparently deciding that at least for the time being there were no jobs available to her. She remarked rather desperately one day that she'd just have to find some other way to get her carpeting. I snapped irritably that there was another way already open to her, and that we'd go get it anytime she wanted to.

Amy looked steadily at me and said, "But I don't want just the carpeting; there are so many things I want, it would never end."

"All right," I said. "Sit down and make a list of everything you want."

Laughing, she turned away and said, "Well, there's not only the carpeting, I also need new drapes, and having the furniture reupholstered— Oh, Jane, forget it, it's just too much."

For the first time sensing victory, I pressed on. "All right, so we'll get new drapes as soon as we've gotten the carpeting, and then maybe by the end of the year, for Christmas, we can buy new furniture."

Her eyes narrowing, as though for the first time really giving it thought, she said, "Jane, are you sure you want to get into all this? I know you don't have all that much money yourself."

"So let me worry about that," I said, smiling. "Certainly there's nothing to keep us from getting the carpeting and drapes right away; then later we'll see about the furniture."

Amy put her hands to my shoulders, holding me off, and we stood for quite some time, looking steadily at each other, then slowly, with a little sigh, Amy said, "Well, all right, if you're sure you want to."

"I'm sure," I said, and leaned forward to kiss her, happy that at last I'd earned Amy's trust — I hoped.

As it was only March, with the taxes not yet paid, I told Amy we'd have to buy the carpeting on time, which I assured her didn't worry me in the least. I couldn't get my hands on that much cash without Russ knowing about it, but I hadn't a fear in the world of taking on monthly payments. And there was no way I'd feel guilty about it. Russ spent more money on beer and wine each month than I'd be spending on this, and Tommy got every last little thing he wanted. I too had every right to get something that I wanted.

"But it's not something for you," Amy said, sighing. "Why don't you get something for yourself instead of something for me?"

"Amy, I love you," I said, grinning, and kissed her again.

We began to spend a day or two a week shopping for carpeting, thoroughly enjoying ourselves—our happiest days. On Monday evenings we went to the lesbian raps at the Gay Center, and occasionally we'd go to the open raps on Wednesday evenings, attended almost exclusively by men. We lunched together, talked for hours, dove into bed to make love, and I'd never been happier in my life; I felt that our every problem was solved, we'd be married for the rest of our lives, and Amy would never leave me now.

One afternoon, after lunch, as we were driving toward a carpet store, I told Amy that I could see only one possible development that might break us up. While I didn't believe in role-playing, in either the gay or the straight world, nevertheless there was no getting around the fact that when two people began a relationship, one was almost sure to be more emotionally secure and assertive than the other, and there could be little doubt that between the two of us I was far more assertive. Possibly, with time, Amy would become more secure emotionally, more assertive, and in consequence the day might come when she'd want to branch out on her own. In time, not content with being loved by me anymore, she might want to go out to find her own sweet, insecure little doll, someone she could pursue, court and win. If this were to happen, I assured her, I felt sure I could live with it.

As I expounded on this theory, Amy, who was driving, kept darting frantic glances at me, blue eyes popping with alarm. Finally, laughing, I said that that was something I simply thought *might* happen, but on the other hand it might not, too.

Once, as we were looking over some carpet samples, when Amy asked my opinion, as she constantly did, I gave it, then added that what I thought didn't matter anyway, she was the one who had to live with it, not I. Dimpling, Amy murmured that we couldn't know that; maybe someday, if we had the thirty-year marriage we constantly talked about those days, I might have to live with it too.

The day we picked out the drapes, agreeing that we'd take the money out of our joint account to pay for them, I touched Amy's arm and said, "This is how, by putting out a little money here and there, I plan to bind you to me forever; you know that, don't you?"

"Promise?" she answered softly, her eyes meeting mine.

Two women happily in love.

When Russ and I were recarpeting, Russ refused even to go look at carpets with me, just as Bob had no interest in going with Amy; but when Tommy and I went, we went to one store only, and spent maybe fifteen minutes there before Tommy had picked what he wanted for his bedroom and between us we'd picked what we'd have for the rest of the house.

Shopping with Amy was altogether different. We went to no less than seven stores, and in each one Amy must have looked at a couple of dozen samples. I began to despair that she'd never find anything to suit her, but finally one day, after our third trip back to the same store, she reached a decision and had the salesman write up the order. About three days later we ordered the drapes. Amy thanked me a hundred times, each time more sweetly, with greater feeling, while I, more than a little embarrassed, kept protesting that there was no reason to thank me at all. Almost entirely against her will, I had talked her into this. Now she couldn't act loving enough, apparently, to repay me for my victory.

The carpeting was installed on a Friday, and it took all day. Early Saturday morning Amy phoned to tell me it was in, sounding terribly excited, then she asked me if I would come down to see it.

When I arrived, Amy let me in and excitedly showed me around the house, talking and laughing. We wound up back in the kitchen, where she offered me a cup of tea, and then remarked, grinning, that so far that morning she hadn't even combed her hair or brushed her teeth. I felt that she had phoned me so early for just that reason, for the added intimacy of allowing me to see her that way, fresh out of bed in her own home, and with such happy excitement sparkling in her eyes. How far we had come from the days when she couldn't even face me without makeup!

One day in mid-April, when we were in my bed together, Amy began to look troubled. With her mouth and chin beginning to tremble, she told me hesitantly that she'd gotten a letter from her mother, who had gone back to live in Bulgaria following the death of Amy's father. Her mother had written that she didn't feel well and hoped that Amy would fly over to visit her, hoped to see her at least once more before she died.

With her voice all but breaking, Amy asked, "So is it — is it all right if I go?"

"Well of course it's all right," I said quickly, thinking, My God, does she think she has to ask me? What kind of a monster does she think I am? "How long do you think you'll be gone?"

Looking relieved, far less frightened, Amy responded airily, "Oh, a year," and I collapsed against her, moaning, saying that in that case I'd die.

"Oh, I'm only kidding, sweetie," Amy said quickly, holding me tightly against her. "Three weeks, or a month maybe, not longer than that. I'll be back in time for my birthday, in June, I promise."

"Well, I'll really concentrate on the book while you're gone," I told her. "Keep myself busy and out of trouble."

"Oh, don't do that," Amy teased. "Go on out and get into a little trouble, I won't mind."

"So if you have a chance to have a little fun over there in Europe," I responded, "don't worry about me, just go ahead."

"Don't be silly," she answered rather tartly. "For me this is strictly a trip I feel I should take; I don't expect to enjoy myself or have any flings."

"Nor do I expect to enjoy myself or have any flings while you're away. As I said, I'll settle down to work on the book."

Early in March I had suggested to Amy that possibly I should write a book about our situation — two married women in love with each other, having an affair. I'd been writing on it steadily for weeks, and while she was gone I'd finish it. That way, as much as I knew I would miss her, the time she was gone wouldn't be wasted.

Amy left for Europe on May 9. From the time she told me she was leaving until the morning she left, she could hardly have been more loving. Whereas earlier in our relationship she had often turned down various invitations I'd extended, told me she was too busy to see me or go places with me, after we'd bought the carpeting and drapes she acted as though she'd forgotten the word *no*, had entirely eliminated it from her vocabulary. She began to say yes so readily to everything I suggested that I soon felt uneasy and more than a little uncomfortable.

"Amy, please, don't ever say yes to something unless you really mean it," I began to caution her. "Don't be one of those people who can't say no."

In a way it was as though I'd accidentally stumbled into heaven, except, as everyone knows, when your every wish is immediately granted, when nothing is ever withheld, you aren't really in heaven, you're in hell. As March gave way to April and April melted quickly away, with Amy's departure date growing ever nearer, I began to feel so uneasy that I could barely cope with it.

Our loving togetherness peaked during the final week of April, the week of my birthday. Amy offered to come over Monday for a session in bed; I mentioned that I'd thought about Monday but had sort of opted for Wednesday, my birthday, whereupon she said quickly, "Why don't I come both days?" We had planned to go to the lesbian rap session that Monday night, but when I mentioned going to the Wednesday-night open session instead, Amy said, "So we'll go to that too." Everything I mentioned she instantly agreed to. Every time I saw her she was meltingly sweet, refusing to cross me in any way, and each time I tried to reason with her about this, she replied that after all this was my birthday; if she couldn't show me how much she loved me now, the week of my birthday — well . . .

We saw each other every day that week, twice for long, incredibly intimate, satisfying lovemaking; we also went out three times in the evening. Nothing seemed to mar our togetherness; every whim I dared to mention was immediately granted. Amy, smiling sweetly, gave in to me on every point. By the end of the week I couldn't take it anymore.

Saturday morning I phoned her and told her that things couldn't go on that way.

"Look, sweetheart," I said, my head aching from the

restless night I'd had, "as a child you were your mother's good little girl, always cheerful, never bad, and as a consequence you spent most of your childhood sick in bed. Then you became Bob's good little girl, afraid to cross him, afraid to feel any anger, never doing anything wrong, and then you spent another twenty years of your life being sick all the time. Now you're all set to be my good little girl, never crossing me, never going against anything I want—Amy, it can't go on, it simply can't."

"Well, if you don't want me to be your good little girl," she replied rather flippantly, though underneath the lighthearted tone I felt that there was a strong hint of panic, "what do you want me to be, your bad little girl?"

"No, I don't want you to be my bad little girl, I want you to be yourself. I want you to get over the idea that you have to be 'good' to earn love. If you keep on the way you have been, always being so goddamn agreeable, you'll wind up sick again, for sure."

"Not as long as I keep on eating right," Amy said, though without a great deal of conviction. "You are what you eat, you know."

"And also what you feel," I countered, "and if you don't have the least idea how you really feel, if you live your life determined to please everyone but yourself, afraid even to think of pleasing yourself— Look, Amy, you've been eating the proper diet for twelve years now, yet aboard ship you got sick."

"Because I had to eat all that trash food they served."

"Food that wasn't all that bad. I ate it without getting sick, and so did everyone else. And then after we got back you were sick again, and spent nine days in bed."

"For the first time in years and years," she murmured, sounding as though for the first time she was opening up, as though possibly I was beginning to reach her.

"Sweetheart, that's just my point. When you were sick then, you kept telling me that you couldn't understand it,

— 168 —

you hadn't had a cold or flu in years. So don't you see that diet isn't the whole answer? Other factors enter in. You simply can't repress all negative feelings and stay well. It just can't be done, at least not by anyone who's as prone to illness as you are."

When our discussion ended some minutes later, I couldn't tell whether I'd made the least dent.

All day Sunday I felt depressed, becoming even more depressed after I phoned Amy to ask if we could have lunch together on Monday. She told me she was too busy to go out, but suggested I come to her home for lunch, the first time she had ever invited me to do so.

I accepted, and Monday at noon drove to her house. Bob was nowhere in sight, but nevertheless Amy acted tense and uneasy. We'd discussed the luncheon menu over the phone that morning, and decided on juice from some green vegetables she had taken from our garden, with fresh-ground peanut butter, unsalted, on unsalted wholewheat crackers.

When I arrived, however, I found that she had changed her mind and was fixing us eggs, which she knew I didn't like.

I didn't stay long. Our first luncheon "date" in Amy's home was not exactly an unqualified success. The way she kept glancing nervously at the sliding glass door to the patio, as though fearful that Bob might walk in on us, kept our conversation superficial, and I felt angry at the way Amy had switched the menu and served me something I'd told her several times I didn't like.

I saw Amy only once more before she left for Europe. When I talked to her over the phone she was reasonably friendly but tense and hurried, always claiming that she was too busy to see me. She was withdrawing again. I hoped it was only in an attempt to deal with the issue with which I'd confronted her, the need to stop being my "good little girl." Surely it would all work out in time, I told myself.

On Friday of that week Amy again invited me over for lunch; twice in one week, when she'd never invited me during all our months together. Apparently, as a step toward greater expression of her feelings, she was trying to integrate me more fully into her life.

Up to then, for the entire year we'd been together, we had lived almost entirely within the penumbra of my life, with my friends, not hers, making love at my house, not hers, and so on. So, while both of us were in a sense leading double lives, my two lives were far more integrated and consequently much less of a strain. Whereas Bob knew about us only what he had guessed, Russ knew just about all there was to tell. Frequently, before he'd leave for work in the morning Russ would ask me whether I was seeing Amy that day, then he'd remind me to make sure we picked vegetables for her. In the evenings, I'd freely, unself-consciously share with Russ anything of interest about Amy that might have come up during the day. At this time Tommy was driving my car to and from school every day. We'd go to lunch or go shopping in Amy's car, and ordinarily Amy would still be at my house a couple of times a week when Tommy got home, though we'd always make sure that we were engaged only in the most casual occupations when he got home. Tommy would walk in, greet us, then excuse himself to go to his room. This was usually the cue for Amy and me to hie ourselves out to the garden to pick her vegetables, ordinarily the last thing we did before she left. I'd walk her to her car, kiss her good-bye, and watch her drive off—no stress, no strain. But for Amy it had worked out far differently.

To begin with, during the early months, her everyday life revolved around her husband, their home, and the friends they shared, and I was simply a secret vice she sneaked off to enjoy when she could. But slowly, as she fell ever more deeply in love with me, grew to trust my love, and we became more and more involved with each other, the emphasis shifted until by the start of the new year she was planning her life around the hours she could spend with me, not the time spent at home. By mid-March she had pretty much isolated husband and home as a tedious burden, to be escaped from as often as possible. Throughout the latter part of March and all of April, she was airily, joyfully racing off to be with me at every opportunity, thoughtlessly neglecting Bob. No longer concerned about being her husband's good little girl, she had thrown herself into the role of being *my* good little girl, until I finally confronted her with it, insisting that it couldn't go on.

Amy took what I'd said very seriously, and as she forced herself to look within, to begin facing her negative feelings, apparently the first one she faced was guilt over what she'd been doing to Bob, which may have prompted her sudden decision to start inviting me to her home.

That Friday when I went to her home for lunch, not only was Bob there but also Amy's married daughter, Jenny, and Jenny's youngest son, Teddy. This was the first time I'd ever met them.

Amy had fixed us baked beans with a green salad on the side, with fresh vegetables from Russ's garden. We all sat down to eat in the open dining room, all family except for me, the intruder, the secret lover!

I had no problem talking easily with Bob, whom I'd always liked and who I felt had always liked me, and I had no problem feeling completely at ease with Jenny and her son.

But while I felt I was sailing triumphantly through the encounter, Amy was so tense and uptight that my heart ached for her. Was she frightened that I'd let something slip out to indicate that she hadn't, after all, been quite the good little wife her husband thought her, quite the good little mother her daughter viewed her as being?

I didn't stay too long after we'd finished eating, and after I said good-bye Amy walked me out to the car. Even then, off by ourselves, Amy seemed scared, nervous, and glanced frequently over her shoulder, as though someone might be spying on us. She was due to leave the following Monday for Europe, and I thought she might need the monthly carpeting payment from me before she left, so I handed her the fifty-dollar bill I'd brought with me.

She took the bill without hesitation, even glancing at it, to see what size it was, murmuring, "Oh, the payment. Thank you, that's sweet," and slipped it into her shirt pocket, but then glanced again immediately at the house as though to make sure no one was watching.

"Well, I—I'd better be getting back inside," she said tensely. "Thanks, Jane, for coming." Then she hurriedly kissed me good-bye and ran back to the house.

I knew by then, of course, that we had serious problems ahead, but I hoped we could work them out.

Driving home, I thought of a brief exchange Amy and I had had the morning after her carpeting had been put in. After she'd shown me excitedly around the house and we were back in the kitchen, I'd mentioned to her that I'd talked to Leslie, who had become a mutual friend of ours, the evening before. Leslie, who had always had an open marriage, had told me happily that she was so enamored of a new man she'd met that she was halfway thinking of leaving her husband.

When I told Amy this, she said, "Doesn't Leslie know yet that you can't find happiness with a man?" which both amused me greatly and upset me.

"Happiness comes from within," I countered plat-itudinously. "No one else gives it to you, it's a do-it-yourself job."

"Oh, of course," Amy said quickly, "I know that." But I wondered whether she really did.

As a child Amy had looked to her parents to make her happy, and only very young children have the right to expect happiness as a gift, it seems to me, and her parents had failed. At eighteen she'd fallen in love with Bob, had married him, expecting him to make her happy, and Bob had failed. Now I felt she had shifted the expectation, the burden, onto me; it was now up to me to make her happy, and, human nature being what it is, I too was bound to fail. As long as she felt she had to *earn* love, which meant she had to repress all anger and please me at all costs, how could she ever be happy?

I didn't want Amy as my good little girl, earning my love; I wanted her to become a self-aware, self-motivated woman happily out to please herself.

I didn't see Amy again until very early the following Monday morning, six-fifteen, when I drove to her house to pick her up to go to the airport. Bob, already up and dressed, led me into the house, apologizing for the fact that Amy wasn't ready yet. He sank down on the sofa, I sat on a chair across from him, and we smiled in a parental, rather patronizing fashion as Amy, obviously nervous and not very happy, rushed around, disorganized, finishing off her last-minute packing. She was leaving us for a month—her very ill, all-too-often-neglected husband, and her hard-to-please, demanding lover—flying off to visit her sick old mother, a woman from whom Amy had spent the better part of her life unsuccessfully trying to win affection and approval. How could she not feel nervous?

At last we were in the car, ready to leave. Without my asking, Amy immediately gave me her mother's name and address, then handed me the passbook on our joint account—in case I had need of it while she was gone, she explained. She had already withdrawn money to pay for the drapes.

At the airport we found ourselves in the middle of a mixup—wrong line, wrong airline, wrong side of the airport—and by the time we caught a ride over to where we were supposed to be and got Amy safely checked in, we had no time left for anything but to say good-bye. Standing on the ramp, facing me, Amy began to cry.

Like a forlorn and guilty little girl, she said beseechingly, "Jane, I love you. Don't be mad at me, please."

"Amy, I love you too, and I'm certainly not mad at you," I whispered urgently in answer, and, holding each other close, we kissed several times.

Before long Amy drew free, picked up her carry-on case, and walked the rest of the way up the ramp, then turned to wave good-bye, tears still coursing down her cheeks.

While I knew there were problems ahead for us, it didn't once cross my mind, as I waited by the window to watch Amy's flight take off, that our good-bye kisses there on the ramp might be the very last kisses we'd ever share.

Thirteen

After leaving the airport, I drove home and went straight to my typewriter to write Amy a letter telling her how much I loved her, how much I already missed her. While I was typing I heard a loud banging on the front door and when I went out to open it I found myself facing a delivery man from a local florist, who handed me a vase with a dozen pink roses in it. Amy's card read: *To my Sweetie, Thanks for everything. Love, Amy.*

A month to get through, without my darling.

Though I missed her almost painfully at first, I soon adjusted and got through the weeks quite happily. I kept very busy, I had Russ and Tommy for company, occasionally I drove down for a lesbian rap session, and Leslie and I went to a couple of NOW functions. I was getting along just fine. There was only one threatening cloud: my increasing awareness that Amy and I were heading toward a very stormy period.

Her first letter to me, written a few days after she'd left, was loving and sweet, but in the postcard that followed, though superficially it was friendly enough, she slipped in a little note of rejection; in the letter that followed that, the hint of rejection was even stronger; and then after that, nothing. No further communication. She'd been gone three weeks by then, and I began to have repeated bad dreams, in which I was crying, or she was crying; she was back but we were angrily refusing to see each other. One nightmare following another, all of them giving me the same, dire message: bad storms ahead.

Though Amy had assured me several times that she'd be back before her birthday, which was five weeks after her flight out, the day came and went not only without her being home but with no definite word as to when she'd return. Though I felt awkward and embarrassed about it, I phoned Bob several times to ask whether he'd heard from her, when he expected her back, but he seemed to know even less than I, to have heard from her even less often. Apparently he was used to this kind of thing when Amy traveled, but I wasn't. I felt frightened, disturbed, and angry. I tried to call but there was no phone, then sent her a wire, but had no way of knowing if it had reached her. All I could do was fret, and wait, knowing that Amy was over there, staying with the woman who had ingrained in her the rigid dictum that one must always do one's duty, that duty comes first, and that one must always pay one's own way and never accept anything from anyone; the mother who had taught her never to face or express negative feelings, who had impressed upon her the need always to smile and be cheerful, who had never given her sufficient love or approval, who had allowed her to grow up feeling "worthless, rotten, and no good."

Still, I'd think angrily, in counterpoint to my fears, Amy wasn't a child anymore, but a full-grown woman, the woman who loved me, and whom I loved.

I quit phoning Bob, fearing to hear him say that Amy was back but hadn't phoned me. Before her departure Amy had agreed that I could see her off at the airport and pick her up upon her return, but I began to feel sure that this wouldn't happen. By now she had withdrawn too far from me. However, I never left the house without leaving a number where I could be reached, just in case Amy phoned from New York to let me know what flight she'd be on. I lived in a state of tension and angry uncertainty, waiting to hear, to have this whole unbearable mess resolved.

Then on a Friday morning two weeks after Amy's birthday, I woke up out of the worst nightmare yet, one so real I felt sick from it. In the dream, so vivid that I was shaking, I stood in front of a blackboard, trying frantically to erase what was written on it, but I couldn't. All I could do was try, while fighting down the tears that choked me, and I knew that Amy was dying. My love was dying, and I felt such loneliness for her that I couldn't stand it. I felt as though I had to get close to her at least one more time, had to crawl into bed with her and hold her against me, feel her against me, at least one more time. Except that I couldn't; she was dying and I had to let go. And no matter how hard I tried I couldn't erase this from the blackboard. All I could do was sob.

As I woke from the nightmare I was filled with the loneliness I'd felt in the dream, a far worse loneliness than I'd ever felt in my waking life for anyone. That empty, sick, lonely feeling stayed with me all morning, a constant reminder of how I would feel were Amy to die. And then, after I'd returned from my weekly grocery shopping, the mail was there. I took it out of the box and carried it in and there was a letter from Amy, mailed locally. I opened it, relieved to hear from her at last, and read:

"Dear Jane,

"I don't really think this will come as too big a surprise to you, as psychic as you are. Bob is feeling so angry (jealous) that he has forbidden me to see you ever again. Please don't come to the house or phone me, forcing me to change my number.

"Amy."

Also in the envelope was a money order for $350, repaying every cent that Amy had taken from me. End of suspense, beginning of storm.

The memory of my dream in which she was dying was still so vivid that her rejection had remarkably little effect on me, in truth was something of a relief. It was so much easier to lose her, possibly only temporarily, to her fears, than to lose her, permanently, to death.

I put my groceries away, phoned Russ at his office to tell him I'd be over in about an hour, then decided that I'd better acknowledge Amy's note at once, via letter, so she wouldn't suffer uncertainty all through the weekend, wondering how I was reacting to her rejection.

In my note I told her I was happy to know she was safely home, was not surprised at her message except for the shift of responsibility onto Bob, which we both knew wasn't true, told her that I had a couple of books of hers I'd return within a few days, and that I loved her and sent her my best wishes. After dropping this in the mail, I drove over, not at all unhappily, to join Russ at his office, which I did every Friday afternoon.

Problem: How to win back a woman who forbids you to phone or come to her house.

Answer: Who knows? Why even try?

I felt I had no choice but to try, not only because I loved her and wanted her back but for her sake as well. Through the closeness, the emotional security, of our relationship, she had begun to open up and face some of her negative feelings, and now she was daring to express them, in withdrawal again, which was the only way she seemed able to. If you can't fight, only flight is left. How could I simply turn my back and walk away, saying, in effect, "Okay, sister, if that's what you want, you're stuck with it"? Surely what Amy wanted, and what I wanted for her, was to become a more completely integrated person, a happy person who knew not only that she was loved but, even more, that she was irresistibly lovable. I didn't want her to be dependent on my love; I did want to help her, if I possibly could, to become so sure of her own worth and lovability, to become so steeped in her own love for herself, that she would be completely free of any need to earn love from anyone else. Surely self-love is not only where it all starts but in most ways also where it all ends.

When I've gone to gay rap sessions and it has come out, often by friends of mine revealing the glorious news, that I am married while at the same time carrying on a lesbian love affair, many times I've been asked, in a friendly manner, whether I consider myself completely bisexual or do I lean more to the straight or to the gay. I always answer, though with a touch of hesitancy, as I feel my answer doesn't really get to the truth, that I lean more to the gay, that now that I've gotten over the paralyzing fears of my youth, I consider myself more of a lesbian.

However, given the chance, I always add that in spite of the two sexual affairs I concurrently enjoyed, I am not really that much of a physical/sexual creature, that my deepest feelings are now, and always have been, maternal. Maternal feelings flow easily and naturally into every relationship I enter, whether with my sons, my husband, my friends, or my sweet, troubled love. If I could be sure that Amy was well and happy, that she had no real need for me, I know I could adjust easily enough to never seeing her again. When I received her brief note of rejection, however, I could not be sure that this was so.

The following Monday, when I wrapped up the two books I had of hers to return them to her, I enclosed the passbook to our joint account, in which I had deposited the $350 money order she had sent me, also $200 as a birthday gift, plus the June payment on the carpeting, bringing the total in the account to just under $900. I also enclosed a friendly, loving letter.

Sometime later she returned the passbook to me through the mail, without any accompanying note.

I phoned her when the passbook arrived.

We talked for about thirty minutes; rather, I talked while Amy listened. Though very quiet and reserved, she was not unfriendly. After the conversation, I thanked her for listening to me and said good-bye.

Russ, who seemed terribly upset by the way things had turned out, announced to me shortly after Amy's note of rejection that, goddammit, no matter how things stood between the two of us, he was going to take her a box of vegetables. Amy had greatly admired his garden, especially all the leafy greens. Months before, Russ had asked Amy whether there were any vegetables she wanted him to grow for her, she had very appreciatively named a few, and Russ had planted them. Now they were ready to be harvested, and Russ, missing Amy's raves about his vegetables, couldn't bear to see them go to waste.

At first I objected mildly to Russ's plan, then decided I had no right to stop him, so I helped him cut, wash, and load a cardboard box of fresh vegetables to take down to her.

A week passed after my phone call to Amy, then another and another. For me the time passed without strain; my dreams were uniformly warm and happy now, Amy seemed very close, and I felt happy. Still, I very much wanted Amy back.

I didn't feel that this was entirely selfish on my part. No one could ever convince me that Amy hadn't been very joyfully in love with me. In addition, I did not want her to have to face a financially uncertain future. I wanted her to have all those things she wanted, all those things that mattered to her. I did not want to abandon her to her fears, cut off from the very things for which she had prayed.

At the same time, *I* needed her. She fit so perfectly into the things that I wanted. I had told Russ for several years that while I hadn't the least desire to get a bigger house, or fancier clothes, or a newer car, the one thing I wanted to do, after Tommy grew up and left for college, was to travel. Russ would never travel with me, I didn't want to travel alone, and here was my beautiful Amy, with her great delight in traveling. Couldn't she see how much I needed her?

I was also very much aware that we were, all of us — Russ, Bob, Amy, and I — being swept very rapidly into old age, with its attendant frailty and disabilities, and the only person I'd ever known whom I could imagine wanting near me, taking care of me when I'm old and ill, is my sweet, loving Amy, who has the gentlest hands, the tenderest touch imaginable.

One morning when I was over at the office, a month after I'd last phoned her, I decided that the time had come to call Amy again. Russ was temporarily out of the office. I lifted the receiver, took a deep breath, and dialed.

When Amy heard my voice she was immediately friendly, rushing to tell me that she was having a lawn sale that weekend, telling me so quickly that I felt it constituted an invitation to me to come to the sale. She then thanked me repeatedly for the boxes of vegetables Russ had been taking down to her, also for a card I had sent her — apologizing for the fact that she had not yet written to thank me for my card — and mentioned that Bob was thoroughly enjoying the crossword puzzles I had cut out of the newspaper daily and had recently mailed to him.

As we continued talking, I asked her why she hadn't yet changed her number, as she'd threatened to do, and she laughed and said, well, I hadn't been bothering her all that much. After all, this was only the second time I had called. Besides, she added brightly a moment later, it costs fifteen dollars to have one's number changed. So I'll send you the money, I said, laughing, and Amy laughed too.

Before long, when, talking and laughing happily with

her, I said, "Oh, Amy, I love you," Amy suddenly became very serious and replied, "Well, we can never get back together now, you'd never trust me again." I immediately agreed, saying that yes, that was true, because of the lousy way she had treated me. Then Amy said, "So why don't you come down here and get me?" and I said, "Is that an invitation?"

"Yes," Amy said, "but be sure to bring a baseball bat with you to hit me over the head, because that's what I deserve for the way I've acted," and we laughed.

When we'd been on the line for almost an hour, I began to feel rather nervous, figuring that Russ would walk back in any minute, or the other line would ring. It seemed a minor miracle that we hadn't once been interrupted by a call during our lengthy conversation. But when I told Amy I'd better go, she kept making conversation, asking me questions, even bringing up recent news events. In time, however, she apparently couldn't think of anything more to say, and we both said good-bye, Amy sounding softly yet insistently flirtatious.

Saturday, the day of Amy's lawn sale, just happened to be the first anniversary of the day we'd gone to the mountains, the first anniversary of our "wedding night." I left the house about eleven, stopped by a florist's, bought a lovely arrangement of a dozen deep-red roses in a vase, and drove on to Amy's house, my heart beating fast. This would be the first time I'd seen her since we'd kissed good-bye at the airport fifteen weeks before, as she'd said to me, tears streaming down her face, "I love you, Jane. Don't be mad at me, please." As though I could really be mad at her!

I pulled up to the curb across from Amy's house, and spotted her at once standing in the front yard. She saw me, and stood there grinning broadly at me, with a slight look of embarrassment. It was a warm summer day, she was dressed in a white shirt and red shorts, her blond hair flying, and she looked adorable. Trembling just slightly, I got a good strong hold on the vase with the flowers, climbed out of my car, took a long, deep breath, and began crossing the street to come face to face with the woman I loved.

Amy had a child helping her, a girl of twelve, whom she later introduced to me as Patty, the daughter of one of her closest friends. This child came rushing over to intercept me as I walked toward Amy.

"Are you bringing those flowers for us to sell?" she asked me excitedly.

"No, I'm bringing them for Amy," I answered, and kept on walking, not to be swerved from my course.

Amy stood near the front porch, unmoving, grinning at me. Her cheeks were flushed, her eyes somewhat moist and apologetic-looking. As I reached her and held out the roses, she said, "I didn't know it was my birthday," her eyes meeting mine.

"It's our anniversary," I said, "our first anniversary." To my intense relief, Amy put out her hands and took the vase from me.

Hurrying over, Patty asked, "But why is she bringing you roses, Amy?" and Amy, tilting her head slightly, smiling just a bit more softly, answered, "Because she loves me."

I know I love her; I know she loves me.

I also know it isn't easy to live — indefinitely — a double life.